Bad Decisions

The Legacy of Lot

Carlton L. Coon, Sr.

Bad Decisions – The Legacy of Lot

By: Carlton Coon, Sr.

Copyright: © 2020 by Carlton L. Coon Sr.

ISBN: 978-1-7356405-0-1

All rights reserved. Written permission must be secured from the author and publisher to use or reproduce any part of this book, except for brief quotations in critical reviews or articles.

Unless otherwise noted, quotations are from the King James Version of the Bible.

Edited by: Pam Eddings

Graphics: SavvyDesigns

Printed in the United States of America

Altered by an Altar

A pre-release read of one chapter of *Altered by an Altar* which will be available for purchase in the Fall of 2020!

Preview Chapter: The Ashes of Yesterday's Sacrifice

At times God demanded an altar. On other occasions, someone voluntarily built an altar. Whichever the case, nothing left the altar like it was when it arrived.

Altered by the Altar looks at what results from altar encounters. To download your free chapter from *Altered by the Altar*:

https://carltoncoon.com/products/free-chapter-from-altered-by-the-altar-the-ashes-of-yesterdays-sacrifice

Light in a Dark Place – Encountering Depression

In case you missed it. This book was written based on life experience. It has been the author's all-time best-seller. All Amazon reviews are "five stars."

Preview Chapter: What's It Like to be Depressed?

Depression is a destroyer, not just in the sense of those lost to suicide. Depression destroys the healthy enjoyment of life. Christians who are depressed may be criticized as "backslidden." Many cannot comprehend the experience of "depression."

https://carltoncoon.com/products/free-chapter-whats-it-like-to-be-depressed-from-light-in-a-dark-place-encountering-depression

Pre-release Reviews of *Bad Decisions – The Legacy of Lot*

Pastor Anthony Mangun – (Pentecostals of Alexandria, Alexandria, LA, USA) I recommend *Bad Decisions – The Legacy of Lot* to any man who wants to lead a life comprised of good and godly decisions. I commend Carlton for the time and study that has gone into his latest. He has done excellent work! The content is challenging and thought-provoking. It brings a uniquely biblical perspective to the process of decision-making. The connection of the scripture "Remember Lot's wife" and the concept of "Remember Lot" is remarkable. This book can be a life-changer for anyone who doesn't just read it - but acts on it!

Pastor DeWayne Butler - (Calvary, Springfield, MO, USA) Any page of *Bad Decisions - The Legacy of Lot* will change lives if people read and apply. This book is jam-packed with life-changing truths. It is an easy read, and the illustrations help the text to flow.

District Superintendent Brian Parkey – (UPCI, MO, USA) Wow! *Bad Decisions – The Legacy of Lot* is a hard-hitting but hopeful book for Christian men. It provides practical advice in every area of life. Well done! I love the questions at the end of each chapter, which challenges the reader to stop and examine themselves in the light of what they have just read. The introduction of *Bad Decisions . . .* pulled me in. Lot's wife is not the story, Lot is!

Bishop Edwin Harper – (Huntington, WV, USA) I have had my mind, spirit, and conscience sensitized because of the surgical autopsy of Lot, in *Bad Decisions – The Legacy of Lot*. The historical results in the lives of Lot's children and their later decisions are a convicting stimulus to the deliberate practices of living and setting precedents for all parents. *Bad Decisions – The Legacy of Lot* should be used in psychology classrooms as a text and study guide for human behavior and developmental counseling curriculums.

Pastor Paul Nightengale – (Townsville, Queensland; AU) *Bad Decisions – The Legacy of Lot* is an eye-opening read on the life of Lot. It should be in every man's toolbox. It is a powerful resource for boys transitioning to men, husbands, fathers, and leaders; I wish I'd had this book as a younger man.

Pastor James Lumpkin – (Member of North American Missions Board, UPCI. Little Rock, AR; USA) I had never given attention to the fact that Lot's wife reflected Lot's decisions. From the first chapter on *Bad Decisions – The Legacy of Lot* was intriguing. This subject is needed. The topics of decision-making or the character "Lot" have been rarely addressed in the entirety of a book. This material is necessary.

District Superintendent J. Stanley Davidson – (UPCI, Gadsden, AL; USA) We live in a world where many refuse to accept responsibility for their actions. But, the law of sowing and reaping is absolute. My friend firmly establishes this point in *Bad Decisions – The Legacy of Lot*. We come to see Lot as someone whose decisions completely damaged his family. Coon masterfully guides the reader through the criteria that go into making correct decisions. I will recommend *Bad Decisions – The Legacy of Lot* many times over.

Chaplain Pam Eddings – (Author/Editor. Chaplain - Greene County Jail, Springfield, MO; USA) – This is your best yet. I cannot wait to hold the finished version. I've been telling my friends about this book.

Pastor Jason Cox – (Stenger, Illinois; USA) On opening *Bad Decisions – The Legacy of Lot*, I planned to read a few chapters and email back a hasty thumbs up. With no attempt at flattery, I read every jot and tittle! *Bad Decisions . . .* is an important book that will appeal to men who aren't usually "readers." Men that sit in pews, rather than seminaries, though it will be good for seminarians as well. The story of Lot is moving and *Bad Decisions – The Legacy of Lot* mines deep.

Pastor Bill Morris – (UPC – Australia, Director of Home Missions - Shellharbour, New South Wales; AU) *Bad Decisions – The Legacy of Lot* is several things. It is incredible, confronting, and gut-wrenching at times. It clearly and openly addresses, necessary, issues that are often hidden from public view.

Pastor Donny Willis – (Westchester, NY) - How do you make decisions? In *Bad Decisions: The Legacy of Lot*, we see how the headline, "Remember Lot's Wife" is a direct result of her husband's decisions. This book highlights the decision-making void in our society and explains how to fill it. It's a call for Christian Men to pick up the mantle of decision-making and lead. Men, your wife, or your children may become the headline. But the decisions YOU make will write the story. If you want to improve your decisions – this book is for you!

Pastor Daniel Bracamonte, (Twitter's *Apostolic Review***)** - Decisions make or break our future. While most teachers tend to use the positive traits of biblical characters, *Bad Decisions – The Legacy of Lot* masterfully draws on the life of Lot to illustrate the danger of bad decisions. Every chapter forces the reader to evaluate their choices in the light of Lot's failures. This book will serve as an excellent reference for pastors who are helping others make better godly decisions.

Pastor Marvin W. Arnold Jr. (Author of *Escaping No Man's Land***)** - *Bad Decisions – The Legacy of Lot* methodically sifts through Lot's self-proclaimed resume and reveals Lot's bad decisions. As a reader, you will finally understand the real reason why Lot's wife *"looked back."* Through his selfishness, Lot recklessly severed all ties with a God-led mentor. It affected Lot's entire family. This book is must-read.

Pastor Landon Decker (Holtville, New Brunswick; Canada) To be candid, the only thing that I would change about *Bad Decisions – The Legacy of Lot* is its geographical location. From wherever the final version now is to my library! This book is a masterpiece. I must have missed something, what is the name of the first book in the God's Men series?

Pastor Art Wilson – (United Nations WAFUNIF Goodwill Ambassador. Detroit, MI; USA) Excellent! With *Bad Decisions – The Legacy of Lot,* Carlton Coon has once again helped the body of Christ with a timely and relevant resource. This book will be a blessing to many as they seek to make better decisions!!"

Table of Contents

Introduction 1

Chapter 1 A Headline Seldom Tells the Story! 5

Before Sodom

Chapter 2 A Casual Commitment 11

Chapter 3 Disrespect is a Decision 19

Chapter 4 Men Who Allow No Father 29

Chapter 5 Benefitting from Your "Chosen" Fathers ... 33

Chapter 6 If "Looks" Decide 39

Chapter 7 Look to the Background 47

Chapter 8 Eclipsed Opportunities 51

Chapter 9 Settling for Mediocrity 57

Chapter 10 Is Prosperity Your Priority? 61

Chapter 11 Yesterday's Memories 67

Chapter 12 Direction Determines Destination 73

Sodom

Chapter 13 Consider Your Risks 81

Chapter 14 Second Chances 85

Chapter 15 Lack of Gratitude 89

Chapter 16 The Decision Never Made 95

Chapter 17 Buying Fool's Gold 99

Chapter 18 Devalued Children 103

Chapter 19 Lot – the Toxic Father 107

Chapter 20 Decisions Under Duress 117

Chapter 21 Consequences of Delay 121

Beyond Sodom

Chapter 22 Nurturing, Empowering and Protecting 129
Chapter 23 Deferred Outcomes 133
Chapter 24 Sodom's Survivors 137
Chapter 25 The Decision of the Second Night 141
Chapter 26 Decisions – as Sand Through an Hourglass 149
Chapter 27 The River of Lot's Decisions 153
Chapter 28 Moab – To Curse God's People............................. 155
Chapter 29 Deliverance from Moab.. 157
Chapter 30 The Wins and Losses of a Man's Life 163
Chapter 31 The Decisions Never End....................................... 169
Other Material by Carlton L. Coon Sr. 173

Introduction

Decision-making is important. What a man decides in the options of life define him. A man's legacy will not differ from the decisions he has made. You cannot plant thorns and leave behind an apple orchard. Therefore, understanding how we make decisions is vital to realizing the implications of both good and bad choices. It is also essential to recognize every decision has implications for you. Further, your decisions impact people in your family, community, church, and generations to come.

Traits of Good Decision Makers

People who make the right decisions combine guidance from God's word, common sense, and their instincts. Good decision-makers:

- Listen to and read varied data about the subject at hand. Reading and listening is the way to be aware of your options.
- Have clear values. These guide the path forward.
- Are open-minded to new ways of thinking and behaving.
- They are willing to change, not stuck in the past.
- Are realistic about possible outcomes. Each decision has both risks and rewards. At times events will not go as was hoped.
- Do not always question their own decisions. They move forward. They treat bad results as a learning experience. (Schmitz, Anna. *"Teaching Decision Making, The Importance of Good Decisions."* ConoverCompany. The Conover Company. Sept 17, 2018. Web. July 4, 2020.)

A man can learn the qualities mentioned by Anna Schmitz. Unfortunately, proud men are often unwilling to learn. They won't learn from others, are reluctant to read or ask questions, or to let the Bible guide. Arrogant men are set up to make bad decisions.

What causes wrong decisions?

- Stubbornness.
- Limited knowledge.

- Lack of wisdom and unwillingness to admit a need for counsel.
- Lack of foresight. Wrong choices often happen if a man considers only the "here and now."
- Selfishness. Such men don't care if their choices hurt others.
- Being confused about what is right or wrong
- Failing to let past mistakes provide an education.

Making the right decisions does not happen by chance. Decisions based on solid God-principles have positive results. Meanwhile, decisions based on pop psychology, contemporary theories, human wisdom, cultural accommodation, or self-interest result in chaos.

Decision-making and God's Will

Decision-making runs the following gamut:

- Straightforward decisions. The Bible gives clear direction. Jesus' will is for you to apply His word. No contemplation is needed.
- When you make a complex moral decision regarding participating in protests, political causes, and interpersonal relationships, the Bible guides, though often in less direct terms.
- "Gray-area" decisions. Biblical examples of these "gray areas" are Bible-era issues of eating meat that had been offered to idols and observing certain days.

Principles for Biblical Decision Making

- Understand that God allows you to choose a course of action.
- Those guided by the Bible are willing to surrender to God, separate from the world's values, and be transformed by the renewing of their mind.
- Obeying God's Word is valued above feelings or circumstances.
- Always consider the impact on others.

(Davis, Billie Ed.D. "Discover It!. *Supplement to Sunday School Counselor*. October 1993. p 3.)

Bad Decisions, The Legacy of Lot, examines the decisions of Abraham's nephew. Right decisions eluded Lot. It should not have been so.

Lot was born into a prosperous family. Lot had ample opportunity to observe how Abram made decisions. Lot was around when Abram did some foolish things. He could have learned from the older man's mistakes. Instead, Lot never learned. In Genesis's last report on Lot, he was still choosing poorly. His decision-making never improved.

No man should follow Lot. Instead, pay attention to how capable men choose, ask them how they arrive at their conclusions. Learn from your own mistakes. By doing these things, your family will have a better outcome than did Lot's. Your right choices will benefit you, your family, as well as your community and church.

** *Bad Decisions – The Legacy of Lot* has content drawn from Jewish sources. Rabbinical thought can be, at times, far-fetched. Those are not referred to here. The ideas included come from multiple sources. Further, at times *Bad Decisions – The Legacy of Lot* gives the bare-bone story flesh, attitude, and a voice. Such imagination claims no divine inspiration. It merely describes what "might" have happened.

Chapter 1
A Headline Seldom Tells the Story!

The headline for the day's bulletin regarding Jesus' teaching read:

Remember Lot's Wife!

Decades ago, a small newspaper's headline read:

Waterproof Man Drowns in Dry Creek.

That is attention-getting. Newspaper headlines don't come from the writer of the story but an editor. In this instance, the editor did a great job of making a play on words.

The story: A man from Waterproof, Louisiana, had drowned. He lost his life in a flooded stream that ran through a community known as Dry Creek. *Waterproof Man Drowns in Dry Creek* was not the story, but those six words are a compelling headline.

In Luke 17, the Pharisees' questions caused Jesus to talk with His disciples about the "day or days of the son of man," (Luke 17:22-37).

Jesus emphasized the need to be prepared. "That day," would allow no hesitation. To convey the seriousness of the message, Jesus said, *"Remember Lot's wife,"* (Luke 17:32). Those three words are a headline. Jesus' warning was – Don't turn back – not for anything.

"Remember Lot's Wife" is not the Story!

As a headline, *Remember Lot's Wife,* (Luke 17:32) gets attention. But just like, *Waterproof Man Drowns in Dry Creek* is a great headline, the headline is not the story.

Lot's wife turning into a pillar of salt is like a snapshot that freezes a moment in time. But the photograph does not express what happened before or after. The phrase, *"Remember Lot's wife"* captures her moment of disobedience. As such, it certainly deserves to be remembered.

The Story Underneath the Headline

But this needs perspective. We do not know the name of Lot's wife. She appears in one chapter telling of the departure from Sodom. Meanwhile, Lot is mentioned 26 times in Genesis. Shortly after Lot's family departed from Sodom and Gomorrah it happened:

> *But his wife looked back from behind him, and she became a pillar of salt.*
> Genesis 19:26

Her failure is quite a headline, "Remember Lot's wife." But what else could we expect? Lot's earlier decisions had positioned his wife to fail. Lot's wife had no control over those decisions.

Jesus' lesson in Luke 17:32 was, "Don't be like Lot's wife. Be prepared and determined to press forward." But there is a story beneath that headline.

The Headline: ***Remember Lot's Wife!***

The Story: ***Lot as a decision-maker.***

Remember Lot?

Jesus never said, "Remember Lot." But we should study Lot and learn from him. Decisions made at life's intersections affect the destination. Lot came to several junctions where he was allowed to decide. In every instance, Lot chose wrong.

Lot – his attitude in traveling with Abram.

    Lot – choosing the well-watered Jordanian plains.

        Lot – in the Jordanian plains, "pitching his tent" toward Sodom.

            Lot – "who dwelt" in Sodom.

            Lot – Rescued and returned to Sodom.

        Lot – In the gate of Sodom.

Lot – Beyond Sodom.

Lot's wife was responsible for her decision to look back. But the answers to the following questions are what positioned her to make one fatal decision.

- How did Lot and his family come to reside in Sodom?
- Why would Lot's sons-in-law choose to remain in a city where destruction was imminent?
- Why was Lot himself hesitant to leave Sodom?

Simple answer: Lot's Decisions

Lot, the man, Lot the husband, and Lot, the father, made terrible decisions.

All that happened to Lot's family, (and there is much to consider) starts with Lot's decision-making. Do, "Remember Lot's wife," her story is now used by conservative Jews to warn children of the danger of disobedience.

But we should also, "Remember Lot." One of history's worst decision-makers.

Lot was not a good husband. In agriculture, a husbandman tended grapes, nurturing them to health and productivity. God's use of the word *husband* in the marriage relationship is no accident. A *husband* is responsible for the healthy development of those under his care. Lot did not nurture and protect his wife. She became what Lot's decisions made her.

Lot's decisions positioned his sweetheart to become entangled with Sodom and Gomorrah. Lot's wife was not the only one affected. His older daughters married men of Sodom. Sodom's perversion and violence were a "norm" for Lot's sons-in-law.

Decisions do not get made in a vacuum. A man's choices – good or bad – build the stage on which his family's history will play out.

Lot's bad choices may compel you to rethink some decisions. You may decide to be more cautious in the future. Your family, your community, and the church need you to be a wise and responsible decision-maker.

Think About It!

1. God has given men the responsibility to be the primary family influencer. The most significant opportunity to be an influencer is at home. Consider your decisions. Do you want your children to repeat them?
2. Would you want your daughter's husband to treat her as you treat your wife?
3. Would you want your daughter(s) to marry a man like you?
4. In what way is your wife's life better/worse for having married you?
5. Someone who is nurturing is supplying care and opportunity for growth. What are you investing that will allow your wife to be a better citizen and saint, as well as mother and wife?

Before Sodom

Chapter 2
A Casual Commitment

Some men are born into privilege. Their family has wealth or influence. Those granted such, do not always recognize their advantage. If you were born into privilege, value the opportunities you receive. Don't waste them. By intentionally building atop your family legacy, your life, and that of your descendants can be more impacting.

Lot had such an opportunity. After Lot's father and grandfather died, his uncle Abram (later re-named Abraham) became the patriarch of his family. In ancient times, a patriarch guided the family. Lot's family patriarch was unique because Abram had heard God call him away from his home city of Ur.

Further, God had promised to give Abram's descendants an area of land known as Canaan. Believing God's promise, Abram left Ur. As Abram's nearest living kin, Lot would have sat near Abram at every meal. He had proximity to a man with a unique relationship with God. A fantastic opportunity was given to Lot. Think about it:

- Lot spent thousands of hours with Abram.
- Lot observed Abram's spirituality and faith.
- Lot saw Abram's faith in action.

If granted Lot's opportunity, what would you do? Would not a wise man have bonded to Abram? It would seem a natural thing to do.

At first, Lot does precisely that. He stayed close to Abram.

> Genesis 12:4: *"...and Lot **went** with him (Abram) ..."*

The Hebrew verb translated *went* describes a **voluntary** action. Lot had decided to identify with Abram's faith and pursuit of the spiritual. Lot joined Abram's grand venture to obtain God's promise.

At least several months pass between the report of verse 4 and verse 5. Verse 5 reveals something different.

> Genesis 12:5: *"Abram **took** ...Lot ...and all their substance that they had gathered."*

The verb translated *took* indicates Lot was now being **forced or coerced** to continue. Lot initially wanted to go with Abram. Now he was being pressured. God was intentional in which words He inspired a writer to use. No word was casual. Between verses 4 and 5, Lot experienced a change in attitude and behavior. God thus inspired Moses to use two different words to describe Lot's participation.

- Lot *went* (Genesis 12:4). He volunteered for the journey.
- Abram *took* (Genesis 12:5). Abram now compelled Lot to continue the journey.

Fickle Commitment

Lot's commitment to Abram's faith and spirituality did not last long. Lot's involvement was grudging. Grudging participation never results in a man's best effort.

Was Lot initially enthused about traveling into the unknown? Being part of Abram's caravan would have been a grand adventure for a young man. But hot days and cold nights, traveling dusty trails across desert and mountain may have eroded Lot's dedication.

Commitment is a decision. But Lot's initial choice to be involved was not his final word on the matter. In time, Lot wanted out.

Fickle commitment happens often. Each day provides another opportunity to abandon or reduce your devotion to the Lord Jesus Christ. Consider your life just now;

> Can it still be said, "He went...," meaning you remain dedicated to wherever God takes you?

> Or, would it be said, "He had to be taken," meaning your participation is grudging?

In times of great enthusiasm, men make public commitments to God. There is nothing wrong with this. Men's conferences, events with hundreds and thousands of people, and compelling church services inspire our commitment to what Jesus is doing.

Then life intrudes. For us, it is not a dusty trail in the Middle East. Instead, our job or the grind of attending early morning prayer becomes an annoyance. Or perhaps we struggle to believe that God will financially bless us if we tithe. Have you ever had an enthusiastic commitment later become an arduous obligation?

Many men have experienced a crisis of commitment. The Bible gives many examples:

- When Jesus spoke of His impending death and the challenges His followers would face: *From that time many of his disciples went back, and walked no more with him,* (John 6:66).
- Paul would celebrate Demas as a fellow laborer in Philemon 1:24. Yet, in the final letter he wrote, Paul sadly said, *Demas hath forsaken me, having loved this present world ...,* (2 Timothy 4:10).

Casual or Committed?

Some men commit to jobs, contracts, marriage, and spiritual life; then later, they abandon their commitment. In "real world living," casual commitment can look like this:

- Despite having a family to support, a man quits a job without having another in hand.
- The gentleman who promised to take his son fishing, but six months later, the trip still hasn't happened.
- A dad who assures his nine-year-old that he will attend her school's lunchtime drama, then yet another "work emergency" renders him a no-show.
- When convenient, the man has his family attend church. But, if an opportunity arises for a day at the lake, his explanation is, "We needed some family time." His comment rings true. But for

some men, that reason is over-used. Every man's family will always need an abundance of God-time.
- "Other things" fill the calendar. These days he attends corporate prayer only when he has a personal emergency.
- A man disciplines his child for being disrespectful. But in the child's hearing, the man speaks ill of his employer, neighbors, other family members, and church leaders.

Where Declining Commitment Is Born

What might have led to Lot losing interest in taking part in Abram's journey? While we don't precisely know, some things are part of human nature.

Disillusioned by difficulty – Many boys who go out for a sport soon quit. The kid realizes practice is not fun. Playing the game is enjoyable, but getting ready to play the game – not so much. The first year of pursuing law or medical degrees is intentionally tough. Those involved in overseeing these fields, as well as educators, prefer a prospective professional "washout" early rather than late. Difficulty can result in a loss of commitment.

Lot started well. Was the travel harder than he imagined? Difficulty can birth disappointment, which often results in frustration. Difficulties will come. Will you refuse to allow any challenge to determine your commitment to God, family, church, and job? Think about it. Just how determined are you to carry out your obligation to:

- Provide for your family?
- Be a robust example of a Godly man?
- Serve your Savior, church, and community in a lasting way?

Time to Deliberate – Genesis 12:5 shows Lot wanting to stop. Had days of journeying given him time to reconsider? While they traveled, did Lot began examining his options? If a man committed to a "God-thing" begins imagining, "But I could…," or "I wish…," he has often started moving away from his original commitment. As you think about the future, are your options filtered through the Bible and your desire to be a Godly man of integrity? They should be.

Mentally, Lot had decided. Did Lot imagine life away from this band of nomads? When Abram coerced Lot to continue, the young man kept walking, but spiritually, mentally, and emotionally, Lot had departed.

Don't be swayed by options that seem more appealing than walking with Jesus. As we will see, what appeals to us is often not as it seems.

Distancing – This is the final step. When Lot was of age and had an opportunity, he abandoned all semblance of partnership with Abram. He distanced himself. Those who leave their commitment will always put distance between themselves and those who remain fully committed.

A Trip To Decommittment

A professional of many capabilities traveled Lot's path. Jeff became unhappy about a decision his pastor had made. He and his wife fretted. In their conversations together, they discussed their frustration. With his wife's support, Jeff began sharing his frustration more openly.

Soon, Jeff and his wife began distancing themselves. Rather than participate in praise and worship, they no longer lifted their hands in praise, and they no longer sang in the choir. They had always sat near the front. Now they drifted to the back of the auditorium. Soon, they were sitting in the balcony. Finally, they left to "help" another church.

That stop did not last long. The couple walked farther and farther into the night. Now, when Jeff encounters a man who has maintained his commitment, he almost runs the other direction. As happened with Lot and Abram, Jeff distances himself from faithful men.

Do you find yourself in any of these stages with God or marriage?

- Does difficulty disillusion you?
- Are you deliberating about your options?
- Do committed people make you uncomfortable?

It is not too late to change your outcome. You need not be a modern-day Lot.

Surviving Your Uncertainty

Know this! Every man has experienced the yearning to "quit." In the setting where Paul mentioned Demas no longer being committed because, "he loved this present world," he spoke of other men. The other men had experienced the same challenges as Demas but did not forsake Paul.

Proper handling of your times of frustration is vital. At any point along the way, Lot could have stabilized his commitment. What are some of the steps a man can take to overcome the seasons of uncertainty? You need to know these because the seasons of doubt are sure to come.

- Mentally and emotionally step back from your struggle. Look at matters as though flipping the calendar ahead 10, 15, and 20 years. What will the future look like if you stay committed? Conversely, what may it look like if you choose a course that does not include God's will?
- When uncertain, look to consistent people. Abram had been rock solid. Lot could have trusted Abram with anything.
- Compare God's promises with the outcome of all other choices.
- Don't let your mind wander! ...*gird up the loins of your mind,* (1 Peter 1:13). In battle, the flowing hem of a soldier's robe was dangerous. It could easily cause him to trip. To eliminate the risk, a soldier would tuck the hem into a belt or girdle about his waist. He had, "Gird up his loins." Pulling up the hem of his robe caused his loins also to be girded up. Peter was saying, "Don't let your mind wander. Stay focused."

Commitment is not Optional

Peter Drucker has trained thousands of people in management and leadership principles. Concerning successful businesses, Drucker said, "Unless a commitment is made, there are only promises and hopes . . .. Creative men have many ideas. <u>But accomplishment only comes through commitment</u>."

Commitment is necessary to excel. There are no sudden successes. Significant accomplishments, including being a good husband, father, musician, singer, employee, or scholar, demand commitment. Jesus understood this. To prospective followers, Jesus said:

> *If any man will come after me, let him deny himself*
> *and take up his cross daily and follow me.*
> Luke 9:23

For a man to "deny himself," he had to eliminate his personal interest and gain from consideration. An example would be for a man to have a part in an estate, but choose to "deny himself" this gain. Jesus was demanding radical dedication.

A man can sustain his commitment through prayer. But your duties are seldom accomplished at an altar. Being "responsible" represents a lifestyle of "being" the right sort of man, and "doing" the right kind of things. Eugene Peterson's book title, *A Long Obedience in the Same Direction*, captures the essence of the dogged determination needed.

Lot started strong. He finished weakly. What about you? Will you finish strong as a:

Husband?
    Influencer?
        Christian?
            Employer?

>Father?

>Employee?

>Servant-Minister?

If you finish strong, it will because you regularly refresh your commitment.

Think About It!

1. If you are young, list the decisions you could make that might destroy your dream. A small decision can have significant implications. Be careful of the choices you make now. Seek wise counsel. Make informed decisions.

2. Of your interests, which could become an obsession? Obsessions are dangerous because they have the potential to become idols. No man can serve two masters. When your attention begins turning into a fixation, go on a season of fasting. Don't read, watch, listen to, or otherwise express interest in NASCAR, football, going hunting, fishing, or reading the Wall Street Journal to learn the nuances of the stock market. Preoccupation with pleasing things can derail a focus on better things.

3. In the middle years, pay particular attention to what is allowed in your mind. The lust of the flesh lives on. When tempted to leave your family, take a realistic look down the road. Write a full page where you imagine how the following relationships will be affected by your departure:

    a. What will your relationship be with your children? Don't imagine it will stay the same.

    b. How will this affect your rapport with current and future grandchildren? Will those living treasures have any stayovers or camping trips with granddad?

    c. How will your relationship with fellow-believers be affected? They love you and desire your salvation. But the camaraderie is unlikely ever to be the same.

    d. What might your future role in the church be?

Chapter 3
Disrespect is a Decision

I can have no more respect for my God than I have for you.
(T.F. Tenney)

Our era may come to be known as the "age of disrespect." Respect for other people is scarce. Disrespect happens even among religious leaders. If this is the case, it indeed happens among all men. In somewhat public forums, <u>small</u> religious leaders deride others. Their behavior eliminates all pretense of holiness. Jesus taught that if a man has a problem with another, he is to go to that man, "one-on-one" (Matthew 18:15-17).

When a person speaks ill of another in any forum, some wise-hearted (and tough-skinned) elder should ask, "Have you personally spoken with that man about your concern?"

A man who consistently disrespects others is not holy. He is likely less godly than if a man decided to wear a speedo swimsuit to lead praise. God's word is clear. Your goal is not to win a debate. Your goal is to "win your brother" (Matthew 18:15).

Lot's second notable decision was to disrespect his neighbors and then the patriarch of his family.

Disrespect devours revival!

Unfortunately, disrespect is a norm in politics, litigation, education, property rights, business, communication, and social media. People do not seek peace; they try to dominate, intimidate, humiliate, and control. God's people are affected.

Given a bit of ground in a man's spirit, disrespect is as invasive as crabgrass. The devaluing of others becomes constant. What respect Paul taught us to practice: Be *kindly affectioned one to another with brotherly love; in honour preferring one another;"* (Romans 12:10).

Family Disrespect

Mark it down! A man who disrespects employees, the disadvantaged, elders, or the arriving generation is an open fire-hydrant of disrespect at home. Home-life is the most massive canvas on which we paint. Behaviors that are tiny brush strokes in another setting become broad strokes of vivid color when a man is at home.

If a man disrespects others in public, that man's family will experience much worse. His children will be browbeaten. Disrespecting words will leave invisible scars. The sledgehammer of intimidation in the hands of a strong man is a fearsome thing. Mental, spiritual, and emotional wounds are inflicted on those who are younger, smaller, and weaker. It should not be so.

>Respect and disrespect are both learned behaviors.

>Respect is a decision.

>Disrespect is a decision.

>You alone decide whether to respect or disrespect.

In Christianity, the abuse of others physically, mentally, spiritually, sexually, and emotionally is seldom addressed. Be clear; men who violate the spirit of their wife or child have sinned. A man who is perceived to be a pillar of the church, but at home, is a petty tyrant, is a bully. No man can both bully and bless.

Such a man's children will almost certainly be lost. If you publicly demonstrate, "loving Jesus, and practicing praise, prayer, and worship," while your family fears open-handed slaps, fists, and harsh words, you are an offender. See yourself as you are. There is no excuse for a man being violent physically, mentally, or emotionally toward his family. It is time to repent. As long as you justify your behavior, there will be no change. Change cannot come until you recognize that your disrespect is ungodly. Christ did not treat any with disrespect.

Confess to your pastor. Why confess to him? Because you will need help breaking the cycle of disrespect. You may want to seek his advice in finding an "anger management" program.

Like depression (addressed in an earlier book – *Light in a Dark Place – Encountering Depression*), the dirty little secret of domestic violence (mental, emotional, spiritual, sexual, and physical) within the church is not to remain unaddressed.

Disrespectful Lot

Lot had little respect for others. Upon arrival in Canaan, Lot did not respect the people who were there before him. Neither did Lot show respect for his children or his uncle. The Rabbi, Braham, wrote that Lot eventually came to see Abram as a failure. Lot had spent decades listening to Abram's stories. Stories about:

- A promised son.
- That Abram's descendants would become a great nation.
- Abram's family was eventually going to conquer and own all of Canaan.

Years passed; Abram and Sarai were old and had no children. Abram owned no land, not so much as a burial plot. Braham said Lot lost confidence in Abram's stories. Disrespect soon followed.

In Lot's material world, Abram's faith was irrational. Abram's obedient faith had produced nothing. Lot was looking at life through the lens of the "now" and the "material." Abram was all about trust. Faith connected Abram to the invisible.

Faith is the substance of things hoped for the evidence of things not seen…
Hebrews 11:1

Did Lot come to have only contempt for this old fellow's ramblings about a promise he had received from an invisible God?

Integrity Abandoned and Authority Disrespected

According to Rabbinical literature, Lot did not limit his disrespect to Abram. Lot instructed his herdsmen to intentionally place sheep on fields belonging to the Canaanites and Perizzites (Genesis 13:7). Lot was stealing his neighbor's grass.

Abram instructed his herdsmen to do the opposite. As Abram honored the rights of others, Lot disrespected those same rights. (Isaacs, Jacob. "Abram and Lot." *Chabad.org*. Kehot Publication Society. Web. July 20, 2019.)

When Lot stole grass, the landowners complained to Abram, the patriarch. Abram confronted Lot about his herdsmen's behavior. But Lot defended his herdsmen and continued sending his flocks where he wanted. (Pesik. ed. Friedman. Targ. of pseudo-Jonathan pp. 9b-10a.)

- Lot said, "I'm my own man. I'll do what I want." A man who becomes an authority unto himself is a danger to himself and others.
- In time, a disrespectful man will yield to no one. He will accept no authority, including the guidance of those who have blessed him the most.
- Lot trampled the rights of others. He was a thief. Disrespectful men do what benefits them regardless of who it hurts. Lot lacked integrity.

Rationalizing Disrespect

You can choose to rationalize almost anything. The *Midrash* is an interpretation of the Old Testament by ancient Judaic scholars. The *Midrash* says Lot's herdsmen justified their use of the fields of the Canaanites and Perizzites. They said, "God gave the land to Abram, who has no heir. Lot will inherit from Abram. Therefore, what we are doing is not robbery."

Disrespectful men give convoluted reasons supporting their actions. On the one hand, Lot believed Abram's promise to be only a myth. Yet when it was convenient to use Abram's "promise" to justify his behavior, Lot did so.

Lot's understanding was wrong. God had promised the land to Abram's descendants, not to Abram. "The Canaanites and the Perizzites were then dwelling in the land." Even Abram did not have a current claim to the land.

If the *Midrash* is correct, Lot presumed to receive an inheritance that would never have been his. God had plans for Abram and Sarai. God's promise still stood.

Disrespectful men commonly have these traits:

- They devalue the needs, rights, investments, and property of others.
- No person can say, "No," and the man obey.
- There is impatience at God's slow, measured way of working. Such people must have "it" now.
- They have an unrealistic view of their importance.

Disrespect Mirrored

Disrespect is not acceptable. Unfortunately, some men gravitate to those whose voice is sharp. Witticisms and innuendo at the expense of others make for easy, though unintelligent laughter. I've not yet known a wise man who appreciated those whose voice had a caustic edge.

Why? They are smart enough to know that when not present, they are the ones spoken of with sharp words. Disrespectful men disrespect everyone. Disrespect has no limits.

Ralph and William

Years ago, a young man, let's call him Ralph, was conversing with a group of peers. Those in the group were saying how much they had gained from a man some decades older. The elder, William, had been kind to Ralph. He had offered Ralph opportunities. If Ralph's name came up in a conversation, William spoke highly of him.

William had considered Ralph as someone who might follow him in a role of some significance. William was brilliant and effective. But

William had a physical oddity. He had a "wandering eye." When William was tired or stressed, one of his eyes would look in a slightly different direction.

As the group discussed what they had learned from William, I overheard Ralph's contribution to the conversation, "But you know there is one thing. When I talk with William; because he has that wandering eye, I don't know which eye I'm supposed to be looking at." Of course, Ralph led the chorus of laughter. The shared appreciation for a good man degenerated into a discussion of the physical oddities of various people these men knew.

Ralph's comment seems innocent. Is it? If the question is, "Did Ralph mean to harm William?" The answer is, "No." Ralph gave no thought to what he said. Therein lies the issue. Disrespecting others is Ralph's normal. Think about it: William, a highly respected man, being spoken of in an affirming way, was turned into the butt of a joke. The relevant questions are:

- Would Ralph want William to speak similarly about him? Every *Ralph* I've known is thin-skinned. They don't like to be the butt of a joke. Such men often go to the proverbial ends of the earth to rebuke someone they imagine disparaged them.
- Would Ralph have spoken in this way had William been present?
- Would Ralph want a man present to tell William what was said?
- Would Ralph want William to hear a recording or see a video of this conversation?

Ralph decided to disrespect William. Some would argue that disrespect is a habit. Perhaps so. But every practice begins with a decision. Tendencies can be changed, and this tendency – must change.

Disrespect's Extended Implications

Until hearing that conversation, I respected Ralph. The overheard conversation gave me pause. Will I ever respect Ralph as I once did?

Unlikely. If Ralph is disrespectful toward someone who magnanimously invested in his life, he excludes none.

There is a second implication. In public, Ralph speaks of his family in glowing terms. Despite Ralph's public words, when they are alone, his family almost certainly experiences unceasing disrespect. Disrespect is not a water faucet that you turn on and off at will. No man who decides to be disrespectful to his peers then treats his wife and children with respect.

Disrespect is a choice. Choose to be consistently respectful. Say a gracious thing or say nothing at all. Even in challenging circumstances, you can choose to treat others with respect.

Those Who Respect Are Respected

No verse is needed to know how the Canaanites and Perizzites would have felt toward Lot. Nobody likes a thief. Again, there is a contrast. Decades later, when Sarah died, Abraham negotiated with another neighboring group, the Hittites for a burial plot, (Genesis 23:3-16). The Hittites lived on the land God had promised to Abraham's descendants.

Those Abram negotiated with, in this matter, respected him. Abram had been a good neighbor. His flocks had not overgrazed the land, and when enemies attacked, Abram fought alongside the Hittites. How differently their neighbors felt about him. Respect given is always respect gained.

Respect is Not Approval

Don't misunderstand. Abraham never became "like" the Hittites. The Hittites were polytheistic. Their homeland was called, "The land of a thousand gods." Their two primary deities were a sun goddess and a storm God. ("What Gods Did the Hittites Worship?. *Answers.com*. web. March 16, 2020) Abraham never worshipped either. Instead, Abraham offered sacrifice and served his God on Hittite land. Abraham did not steal their grass. Neither did he battle against the Hittites over their worship of false gods. Abraham respected the Hittite's right to be wrong.

Abraham's descendants would later conquer Canaan, but he respected the Hittites' current rights. He even paid for a burial spot for Sarah. Like Abraham, we can treat others with respect while not condoning their behavior.

Respect Given is Respect Returned

As Abraham negotiates the purchase of a burial plot, one phrase shines out. The Hittites acknowledge Abraham, calling him *"a mighty prince among us"* (Genesis 23:6). Abraham had respected the Hittites. In turn, they held Abraham in high regard. A man who treats others with respect, no matter how much he disagrees with their lifestyle, attitude, disposition, addiction, or theology, will receive honor in return.

We can also see how much respect the residents of Sodom had for Lot. Lot's neighbors ignored his effort to defend his guests. Instead, the men of Sodom spoke of him with sarcasm, (Genesis 19:9)

Based on what you know about Lot's treatment of Abram, the Canaanites, and Perizzites do you suppose he treated his neighbors in Sodom with respect? It seems unlikely that Lot, who disrespected even Abram respected his new neighbors.

How to Be Respectful

This section should be unnecessary, but it isn't. Few receive training on *how* to respect others. But, every man can learn how to honor his family members, neighbors, fellow-worshippers, pastor, and local church leaders.

Our youngest son, Chris, attended Truman Elementary in Springfield, Missouri, USA. While in the fifth grade, Chris came home one day and told his mom, "My teacher needs a 'put-up' class." Not understanding, Norma asked, "What do you mean, 'a put-up class'?"

Chris said, "All she does is 'put us down.' She needs to attend a 'put-up' class. It will teach her how to put us up instead of put us down." Many people need to visit a "put-up" class. Start respecting others by being a man who "puts-up" rather than "puts-down."

It takes little effort to respect others. Richard Stoppe's writing included what he called the *Ten Commandments for Showing Respect*. (Stoppe, R.L. *Leadership Communication*. Pathway Press. 1987.) Stoppe's list is adapted a bit.

1. <u>Respect yourself</u>. Respecting the personality, rights, and differences of others grow out of appreciation for your uniqueness. *Be comfortable in your skin.*

2. <u>Listen, hear, and understand</u> what those close to you are saying and feeling. Encourage others, especially your children, to speak freely, openly, frequently, and with liberty. *Encouraging this sort of communication gives you the chance to teach them how to express themselves to others with all due respect.*

3. <u>Accept others</u> regardless of their peculiarities. Consider their ideas, suggestions, opinions, and feelings. Give positive feedback when a person does anything well. *As our Chris said, "Learn to 'put-up.'"*

4. Show that you <u>believe in the dignity of all labor.</u> God knows no menial jobs. Regardless of a man's job, treat him with honor, deference, appreciation, and equality. Show the same basic human respect for a man bussing tables as for your pastor or boss.

5. <u>Spend time participating in the activities and interests of your closest relationships.</u> Move beyond social amenities to where you know others more deeply. *Such in-depth knowledge may mean fishing together or playing board games. It will most definitely require you to invest time.*

6. <u>Refuse to be manipulative.</u> Don't use people as dispensable pawns. *Don't push other people's buttons through their fear or*

insecurity. The advice to "stop manipulating," is particularly true in respecting your wife and children.

7. <u>Don't control or smother those near you.</u> Give room for freedom, learning, growth, and interdependence. Your wife particularly needs this. Though the two of you are one body, you each have your abilities and individual goals. *A good husband wants to see his wife fully develop her talent and skills. If in old age, a man's wife is a bitter crone, the finger of blame will undoubtedly point to her husband. He made her what she is.*

8. <u>When criticism is necessary, address only the behavior</u>. Never demean another person. Phrases like, "You are stupid," or "How could I have fathered someone so dumb," demean. *Such comments do not address the behavior; they attack the person.*

9. <u>Refuse to put others down</u>, *even when others do*. Don't put people in their place. *Support and build people rather than destroy them.*

10. <u>Give positive strokes when possible.</u> *James Dobson said a parent needs to give children seven positive strokes for each negative comment made. Dads, be mindful. Start keeping score!*

Think About It!

1. Rabbis say Lot did not respect Abram because of his age and because God's promise had not come to pass. Like Lot, our society gives little respect to many of those who are older. How could you do better in respecting your elders? How can a church be effective in making sure elders are valued?

2. Do you know someone like Ralph? Why do you suppose the *Ralphs* of this world act as they do? Wise people do not seem to take to Ralph, with his sarcastic disrespect of others. Why do you suppose this is the case?

3. Does anything come to mind that should be added to the *Ten Commandments for Showing Respect?*

Chapter 4
Men Who Allow No Father

> The fathers we choose are more important
> than the fathers we are born to.
> (Unknown)

When Abram realized Lot lacked integrity, he felt the need to put distance between himself from his nephew.

And Abram said unto Lot, Let there be no strife, I pray thee, between me and thee, and between my herdmen and thy herdmen; for we be *brethren. 9Is not the whole land before thee? separate thyself, I pray thee, from me:... 11Then Lot chose him all the plain of Jordan...,* (Genesis 13:8-11).

In letting Lot choose first, Abram acted against his self-interest. Imagine you and a friend receiving a grant of two pieces of property. Each of you will become the owner of one property. One plat of land is 10 acres of beautiful farmland, the second a ¼ acre in the desert. If you tell your friend, "You choose first," what will likely happen? Your friend will choose the 10 acres. In allowing him to make the first choice, you have acted against your self-interest. Abram did precisely that.

In seeking counsel, it is wise to get counsel from someone who has no self-interest in the outcome. In the case of Lot's decision on where to go, Abram's ambitions were not in consideration. Since Abram had no self-interest, Lot could have trusted Abram's advice. Instead, Lot counseled only with himself.

To "choose a father" is to select someone whose life pattern you can envision following. Who do you watch, and to whom do you listen? Choose such influencers with thoughtful intentionality. Lot had a deserving "father" available. Abram's life was worth imitating.

Lot did not seek Abram's input. Lot was doing this "on his own." Lot was not of that unfortunate group who have no real man in their life. But, Lot chose to ask Abram no questions or invite suggestions.

Lot noticed only the well-watered plains. He could imagine healthy sheep and cattle. Lot had "dollar signs" in his eyes; prosperity and ambition were his blind spot. Prosperity and ambition are the blind spot for many. Abram would have offered a different perspective.

You seldom lose by seeking wise counsel. Lot exemplifies the determinedly independent man who will have no advisor, no father, and often no pastor.

The Obvious May Not Be Correct

For Lot, the obvious did not prove to be the best. It is often so.

The prophet Samuel was sent to the home of Jesse in Bethlehem to anoint a king to follow Saul. While there for a feast, Samuel saw Jesse's oldest son Eliashib. Eliashib had the kingly traits Samuel imagined to be necessary. He immediately assumed Eliashib was the one he had come to anoint. God had other plans. When a decision seems obvious, we tend to act without further thought.

An executive with whom I worked would often bring up, "The Law of Unintended Consequences." Unintended consequences happen when you do not take a 360-degree look to consider four things:

- What are the long-term implications of my action?
- How will this decision impact others?
- What precedent will this action set?
- Where will this path lead if followed to its likely destination?

Silent Patriarchs

A young man became pastor of a significant church. During the process of becoming the pastor, it was his repeated desire for the former pastor to be the church's "bishop" and his pastor. In truth, he had something different in mind. In short order, he eliminated the "pastoral voice" from his life. He asked only a few questions, and soon none at all.

Instead, he sought the input of an esteemed elder, then it was a district superintendent, and in time, the pastor of a larger church a few hundred miles away. Soon - there was no voice. Any time someone challenged his thinking or offered an expanded perspective, he muted the sound of that person's voice.

Like Lot, he chose to have no father. Today, his life is a train wreck of "success" mingled with anger. Moral turpitude is the norm, and his family life sits on the edge of violence. Spite and marital resentment fuel the actions in his family. The marriage endures, but only for the sake of the material things and the "fame" short-term success has brought. Each day, Sodom draws nearer.

Are you such a man? Stubbornly, and at times "stupidly" self-willed. Is it said of you, "Nobody can tell him anything?" If so, repent and wise up. Every man needs help. We all have blind spots.

Take a moment to evaluate. Is there a "father" who can tell you, "No," and you grudgingly obey? Or, have you silenced those voices?

Why Do Men Reject Fatherly Influence?

Every such man has his reasons. Several are present in Lot.

- Ambition. The well-watered plains seemed to guarantee success.
- Perhaps Lot remembered the comforts of Ur and saw similarities in the sizable city of Sodom.
- The desire to be his "own man." With Abram no longer present, Lot became the patriarch for his immediate family.
- Lot was affected by the desire of the eyes.

Most men desire independence. That is good. But there is a difference between being independent and abandoning counsel. If a man listens to a "fatherly" voice and still chooses the well-watered plains, he has at least received advice on what awaits.

Everything on the list that may have motivated Lot has its origin in pride. Decisions driven by pride do not turn out well.

Pride goeth before destruction and an haughty spirit before a fall.
Proverbs 16:18

Think About It!

1. Have you ever made a decision, and in time thought, I wish I'd talked with someone about this? What was the situation? What was the outcome? Looking back, who do you feel could have given you good advice? Why would that person have been a benefit?
2. Norma and I purchased a business some decades back. It seemed exactly right. It fit her passions, and we were in missions needing secular employment to make ends meet. Except we didn't know the right questions to ask. Soon, we were in a mess. What questions need to be asked if someone is buying an existing business? What professional help should we seek in decisions of such a magnitude?
3. Men are creatures with an ego; God made you that way. But ego and ambition can result in arrogance. What can a man do to protect himself from his ego, pride, and arrogance?

Chapter 5
Benefitting from Your "Chosen" Fathers

Several years ago, a young pastor phoned and asked me to be his "Bishop." I told him I'd pray about it and for him to call me in one week. In prayer, it seemed right. When he called, we had an extended conversation about our mutual expectations.

In my experience, the pursuit of wisdom and information came from the protégé. No mentor has yet chased down someone in hopes of influencing them. So the burden was on him to contact me. If directed by the Holy Spirit, I'd contact him. He told me of his shortcomings and what he'd like to learn. It fit, I felt there were ways to be of benefit. The conversation ended with a sense of covenant followed by prayer.

I've never heard from the fellow again. Perhaps I misunderstood the Lord. I've done so before and will again.

But maybe the Holy Ghost was clear, and there was no misunderstanding. Gaining insight from others takes effort.

How to Ask for Counsel

In speaking with your "Abram," tell him your situation and the various options. Ask for his advice from his experience and observations. You want him to warn you about the dangers ahead.

The benefit of counsel comes to those who listen, open their eyes to potential danger, apply, and at times imitate their "chosen father."

Choosing Your Advisers

The voices you heed are critical. In seeking counsel, don't go shopping for someone who will tell you what you want to hear.

- Not the guidance of those who tend to nod their head in agreement but are not given to thought.
- Not the counsel of your age group. The elders of Israel cautioned Solomon's son Rehoboam. But his contemporaries

encouraged him in folly, (1 Kings 12:6-14). The counsel of Rehoboam's peers caused him to lose over 75% of his kingdom.

- Not the input of sycophants who will tell you what they think you want to hear.
- Not the counsel of a fellow who is bitter over some real or imagined slight in life and has a vendetta against a person, church, employer, or someone who offended him.

It is wise to seek counsel from "graybeards," those with a hoary (gray) head of wisdom (Proverbs 5:1-2; 16:31). The same writer said there is benefit from a "multitude of counselors" (Proverbs 11:14; 15:22). Lot's choice seemed so obvious that he felt no need for help. Learn from Lot, ask counsel even when a decision seems obvious. Ask a wise elder to offer thoughts about your options.

Be an exceptional man! Welcome voices that represent years of experience. Their wisdom will broaden your perspective. Ask elders to inform you of any potential danger. Would Abram have warned Lot about taking incremental steps toward Sodom? Might Abram have suggested, "Lot, you can move to the plains, but don't EVER decide to reside in Sodom and Gomorrah?" Lot never knew Abram's thoughts because Lot never asked his opinion.

Voices to Ignore

In choosing someone to help navigate the difficulties of marriage, don't select:

- Someone thrice divorced.
- A man you know is unfaithful to his marriage vows.
- The fellow who publicly speaks ill of his wife.
- A man who is controlling while the couple is in public. He is a bully. You don't want to think or act like him.
- The man whose wife earns the family living, while, without good reason, he does nothing.

In choosing a man from whom to learn how to be a better father, don't select:

- A man with no children.
- A father who says words such as "Dummy" or "Stupid" in referring to their child.
- The dad who has never attended his daughter's music recitals.
- A dad who caters to a child's every desire.
- A man who does not discipline his children.
- The man whose child can do no wrong. Rather than support the child's principal or pastor in a difficult situation, this fellow always defends his kid.
- A father who always says, "Yes," or a father who always says, "No."

Choose a hard-working man who pays his bills. The "father you choose" should have faith. Watch such a man. Ask questions; apply what you see and hear.

For the Man Who was "Raised by Wolves"

In childhood, some men's only male influencers were violent or abusive. A friend is such a man. He has been in and out of jail, and addiction has darkened his life.

As an adult, he has had one live-in relationship after another, along with several attempts at marriage. But, Sim did not get where he is without help.

He was born to an addicted mother. She was so promiscuous that Sim's father is unknown. While Sim was in elementary school, he arrived home one day to learn that his mother had abandoned him to the care of the state. Sim's threadbare clothes and a toy or two were thrown in a green trash bag. It was all Sim could take with him.

From that day on, Sim bounced from one foster home to another. He was an angry boy; none could handle him for long. Sim was beaten and experienced abuse of every kind. As Sim got older, new horrors added to what he had already endured.

A friend says of Sim, "He was raised by wolves."

Sim's life has not all been sordid. Decades ago, Sim was "born again." Jesus worked in Sim's life. A church that actively loved him became the family Sim had never known.

For the first time, Sim spent time with godly men. Sim's difficult childhood had not affected his mind. He was brilliant. Sim was wise enough to observe how "real men" acted. After Sim listened to mature men pray, he mimicked what he heard. Sim saw patterns of consistency. He applied those toward learning a trade and pursuing an advanced college degree.

Sim had been "raised by wolves," but as a young adult, he selected his influencers. Such a choice is the making of many a man.

If your life has been like Sim's, don't muddle your way through. Connect with men who are doing something with their lives. You can break this cycle.

- Live for God hard. Don't be on the edge of His church. Be a man of praise, worship, Bible study, and prayer.
- Watch how a Godly man treats his wife and kids.
- Notice the work ethic of good men. Unless there is a dire reason, they stay employed.
- Observe them as they give their tithe and offerings.
- If an opportunity comes, ask how they budget their finances.
- Listen to men who know how to pray. Imitate their prayer life.
- Such men are consistent in attending church. Do the same!

Above all else

Ask questions! Lots of questions.

Seek opportunities to "hang out" with good men.

When you are with them, listen more than you talk.

Mentor/Protégé Relationships

The idea of "fathers we choose" may need explanation. Men often say, "I don't have anyone to be my mentor." That statement indicates a misunderstanding of mentor/protégé relationships.

A "father" need not be someone with whom you often visit. In an ideal world, that would happen. But that seldom works out. Beyond my own godly Dad, three men became mentors. It was decades before I had a close personal relationship with two of those men.

Yet, they trained me. I learned by watching the two men's priorities and behavior. When an opportunity came, I would ask questions. Often my questions were asked during a brief phone call. Later, the interaction was by email or text. Seldom did we sit down to have a conversation.

In choosing influencers, begin by observing the principles that guide effective men. Then apply those principles to your life. A novice woodworker learns to turn wood by watching a skilled artisan. You do the same.

Whatever Lot may have learned from Abram was never applied. What a fool! Don't be that sort of man.

Think About It!

1. List two men from whom you might seek counsel in the areas listed below. Be sure to make your choices using the filter of those from whom or whom not to seek advice.

   - Your career.
   - Concerning purchasing or starting a business.
   - Managing your money to budget and save for the future.
   - Marital difficulties.
   - Sexual temptation.
   - Your child's teenage years.
   - Stepfamily challenges.

- Being consistent in personal devotion.
2. Do you know of anyone who has ever sought advice from a person who was not qualified to give it? If the man took that advice, what was the outcome?

Chapter 6
If "Looks" Decide

"One look" was all it took for Lot to make a significant decision! Over fifty years ago, *The Hollies* recorded a song about love at first sight:

> Just one look, that's all it took.
> Baby, just one look!

You seldom get reliable information from "just one look."

When Lot was wealthy, he not only had a dispute with his neighbors. There was also conflict between the herdsmen of Lot and Abram. Abram realized the situation was not going to improve and made Lot an offer:

> *⁸And Abram said unto Lot, . . . ⁹Is not the whole land before thee? . . . if thou wilt take the left hand, then I will go to the right; . . .. ¹⁰ And Lot <u>lifted up his eyes, and beheld</u> all the plain of Jordan, that it was well watered every where, . . ., even as the garden of the LORD, like the land of Egypt, as thou comest unto Zoar. ¹¹ Then Lot chose . . ..* (Genesis 13:8-11)

Lot lifted his eyes and beheld.

    Then Lot chose

Lot did not take a closer look, nor did he question those who had been to the well-watered plains. Lot did no research. He simply beheld and decided.

And Lot mentally inflated the value of what he saw. The plains of Jordan are impressive compared to the rocky hillsides overlooking them. But Lot saw something that was not there.

It looks like the "garden of God" (Genesis 13:10)

Lot saw the plains but imagined Eden. Lot converted what he had heard about Eden to the Jordanian plains lying before him. In Eden:

- The bees did not sting.

- There was no sweaty labor.
- Lions did not threaten humans.
- Weeds did not choke productive plants.
- Cities rife with sexual perversion, and violence did not exist.

The well-watered plains were nothing like Eden. The bees stung, success required sweat, wild animals were a threat, and the grass of the Jordan River valley had plenty of weeds.

Lot decided before he had complete information.

>He decided having asked no questions.

>>He decided based on a "pie in the sky" fantasy.

Lot was a poor decision-maker.

Good decisions result from thorough information. Most decisions require facts, and excellent decision-makers tend to drill beneath the obvious. They then deliberate. This sort of decision-maker never buys oceanfront property in North Dakota.

How can you be a better decision-maker than Lot? Do some diligent work before you decide.

1. What choices exist? Be realistic about your options. Without training, you'll not find a job as an underwater welder. There is no need to look at those job listings. Be sensible.
2. Research the options. Knowledge enables wisdom. Don't make unlearned decisions when information is available.
3. Before you decide, pray for God's direction. By the way, praying for God's guidance is not the same as asking Jesus' blessing on what you have already decided.
4. Does the Bible have anything to say on the topic? If it speaks specifically to the issue or addresses the principle, then apply the Bible truths. Seek no other counsel. "God said it! That settles it." Deciding by your "look" rather than "God's book" will result in trouble.

5. On paper or screen, list the pros and cons of each option. What is good or bad about each alternative? Looking at both will keep you from imagining that you are getting a "Garden of Eden."
6. Never decide for something you do not understand. Apply this advice to investments, insurance, and changes in doctrine.
7. Mentally walk through the long-term outcomes of each option. Imagine the benefits of things going well. Imagine what the result will be if things go wrong.

"Then Lot chose...!"

Lot chose based solely on what he saw. Abram acted on the promise he had heard from God. Having listened to God, Abram believed for the invisible and sought it.

In part, the words *believed* and *beheld*, define Abram and Lot. Which most closely describes your approach to life? Do you trust God's promise, knowing you will eventually experience it? Or, are you motivated by what you can see? On three simple words hangs much of Lot's history. This is true for many.

- Then Lot chose.
- Then Carlton chose.
- Then Samuel chose.
- Then _____ chose.

Lot's choice started a slow-motion disaster, setting his wife up to disobey God and become a pillar of salt. Lot's two older daughters died in the fire and brimstone of Sodom and Gomorrah. His younger daughters were left scarred by Lot's moral choices.

One choice today can determine the outcome of many tomorrows, not all of them your own. Don't decide based on "just one look."

The Power of a Look

Men are influenced by what they see. Visual stimuli affect men far more than women. It was the case for Lot, but not just for Lot.

- Herod, the tetrarch of Galilee, watched his stepdaughter, Salome, dance. He promised her up to half his kingdom. She asked him to kill John the Baptist (Mark 6:19-20). Just one look!
- When Israel conquered Jericho, the soldiers were to take nothing of value. A man named Achan disobeyed. Achan's confession reads: *"When I saw among the spoils a goodly Babylonish garment, and two hundred shekels of silver, and a wedge of gold of fifty shekels weight, then I coveted them, and took them…,"* (Joshua 7:21). The result, Achan was later stoned to death. Just one look!
- David saw a beautiful woman, bathing. Undeterred by her having a husband, David seduced her. To cover-up, David arranged the death of her husband. (2 Samuel 11) Just one look!
- Now, you fill in the blanks from your experience or observation: _____(the name of a man – yourself or another) beheld _____(what did the man see) and _____ (what did the man do?)

A Look and A Choice

Herod's look at Salome impressed him. Herod *chose* to assassinate John the Baptist. Achan's look at the Babylonish garment, 200 hundred shekels of silver, and 50 shekels of gold awakened materialism. Achan *chose* to take them. David's look at Bathsheba stirred sexual desire. David *chose* to seduce her.

Lot's look at the well-watered plains triggered ambition. Lot *chose* to journey east.

The rest of the story for the, "Just one look" guy in *The Hollies* song is unknown. If that fellow's one look had the same outcome as those taken by Lot, Herod, David, and Achan, it did not end well. Don't make your decisions based on one look or even two.

Eye Trouble

"Eye trouble" has never been eradicated. Millenia, after Lot, John specifically addressed the continued danger of wanting what we see.

> *For all that is in the world,... the lust of the eyes,...*
> *is not of the Father, but is of the world,* (1 John 2:16).

The Greek word translated "lust" means *desire*. Men are lured by what they see. Most men, if not all, have "eye trouble." How does it affect us?

- You did not want a new boat *until* you saw what *Bass Pro Shop* had on sale.
- You could not imagine being unfaithful to your wife *until* you saw the "come hither look" on the new coworker's face.
- Your truck with 200,000 miles on it was satisfactory *until* you saw an advertisement informing you that Ford would sell you a new vehicle at 0% interest for nine years.
- An iPhone 6 worked well *until* you saw the features on a friend's iPhone 10.
- You think gambling is a fool's play *until* you learn the lottery is currently worth $5,000,000.

Living with Bad Eyesight

Eyeglasses, contact lenses, or surgery can correct poor vision, God's word and wise counsel can correct a man's poor eyesight. But you have to trust those corrective lenses.

- Perhaps you are offered a higher paying role that will hugely reduce family-time. Since your daughter is at a time where she needs much affirmation from her father, your wife has asked you not to take the job. What now?
- You get emotionally involved with a coworker. You say, "We've done nothing wrong. We are just good friends. I've never touched her." But after expending your emotions on your "friend," you are emotionally bankrupt. What will you do?
- Do you regularly move from one church to another? In each church, you soon see something you dislike. The grass looks greener elsewhere. Because of continually being transplanted,

your children have no spiritual roots. Will you stop looking for the bad at your current church?

Your Eyes and Sexual Temptation

Eyes are a door to our brain. Sexual temptation comes through your eyes. A co-worker who dresses "hot" and drops suggestive hints seems ideal, especially since your home life is a bit stale. Your eyes behold, and your brain says, "Go for it, you may never have such a chance again."

Men must take measures to protect their eyes. In our over-sexed society, only by moving to a mountain without media access can you avoid the lurid. Sex sells, and advertisers know it. The scarcely clad female form gets immediate attention.

Sexual intimacy, no longer being sacred, makes matters worse. Some people treat sex as though it were a handshake, and these days, pornography makes house calls.

Our world has abandoned scruples regarding fornication. Fornication is a Bible word covering improper sexual relations, including adultery. But, sex outside marriage has been normalized on the screen and in print. But not to God. And lest you fool yourself by deciding to act on what seems so available – sexual sin costs like no other transgression. To the most sexually engaged church of his era, Paul wrote: *Flee fornication. Every sin that a man doeth is without the body; but he that committeth fornication sinneth against his own body,* (1 Corinthians 6:18).

Having an affair or divorcing your wife may seem like a "garden of Eden." It is not! Do either, and you sin against your own body.

In time, you discover that what you imagined to be Eden has the pungent sulfuric smell of Sodom. The new lady has morning-breath. She may not be able to boil water or fry an egg. Her sexy lingerie will disappear; traded for a threadbare robe like the one your mother wore.

The woman you imagined to be ideal – "like the Garden of Eden," will be a garden of thistles and thorns. Your ideal turns into an ordeal. She may be a vengeful woman who is a hellcat when you are with her all the time.

In Job's distress, he did not want to further complicate his life. He said: *I made a covenant with mine eyes; why then should I think upon a maid?* (Job 31:1).

I've advised men who were enticed by what they beheld. Most have ignored every warning. <u>None – not one – ever - of those relationships has worked.</u> Job's principle would benefit all.

How would a covenant with your eyes read? A pastor friend teaches men to never look below a woman's neck. Establishing such an agreement with yourself will be a start to protecting you from your eyes.

What Lot envisioned as the "Garden of God" was the first step toward disaster. Don't let your look decide. Don't entertain notions of the forbidden. In this, God's Word has chosen for you. No decision is required.

The Trickle-Down Effect

If you decide to move on because of what you have beheld, the outcome will have unimagined ramifications. Remember, no decision happens in isolation; there are repercussions. Unanticipated consequences follow.

- Your ex-wife suffers an inevitable attack on her self-esteem.
- Depression settles on your kids.
- Your children's resentment toward you may well impact your relationship with them for the rest of your life.
- Grandchildren – both your own and those of the new wife – may well be a step-removed experience. You are more of an uncle, seen on occasion, than a beloved grandfather.

- When grown, your children, are more likely to go through multiple marriages.
- Your integrity will take an inevitable hit in the community.

Lot decided because of what he *beheld*. Don't allow the look of things, no matter how attractive, to make your decision.

Think About It!

1. What have you done to protect yourself, your home, and children from the onslaught of readily accessible pornography?
2. As a mental exercise, imagine sitting down to tell your children and your elderly parents of your moral infidelity. Imagine telling your children that you are divorcing their mom because you have found someone new. What feelings do you imagine will arise as you share those words?
3. What Lot considered significant had a lasting impact on his wife and children. How will your priorities impact your children?

Chapter 7
Look to the Background

The Jordanian plains lay close at the foot of the mountains. Lot lay in the distance. Could Lot see that far? Nothing indicates Lot noticing what lay "out there."

The decisions you make today, this week, this month, and quite often this year are the foreground of life. It is the immediate future. At times, men make quick decisions without looking at what lies "out there." How many decisions are made without considering life ten years from now? Can a decision made when your son is seven years old, affect him as a young adult? Certainly!

Vincent Van Gogh may be history's most famous landscape artist. Landscapes consist of a "foreground" and "background." Such art presents a grand view. One of Van Gogh's most famous works, *The Starry Night*, can be viewed from several perspectives. In the foreground is a jagged rock, framing a church with homes nearby. Mountains overlook the village.

Meanwhile, Van Gogh's background for *The Starry Night* is swirls of vivid color depicting stars overlooking the tranquil scene. Like Van Gogh's painting, life always includes a foreground and background.

Life in the Foreground

The stars in Van Gogh's sky did not cook dinner for any people living in the tiny homes in the foreground. Nor did the stars preach a sermon in the village church. The front of Van Gogh's painting is where daily life happened. But the title, *The Starry Night*, focusing on the distant view, shows Van Gogh's priority.

You live in the foreground of your life.

- It is returning to work tomorrow.
- Changing the oil.
- Deciding to take the overtime hours.

The necessary things of life are dominant. The foreground requires immediate attention. Who has time to consider the stars when there is a lawn to mow? Our interest in the urgent minutiae of life can cause us not even to see the horizon.

Consider the Background

Eventually, bad things happen if your engine oil is not changed. Sooner or later, bad things happen if your children don't have godly influences. Simple things matter:

- A monthly date with your daughter, where you make her feel like a princess.
- An outing to ride go-karts with your son.
- Participating in your church's praise and worship.
- Being sure your children hear you pray.

On a given day, these may seem insignificant, but the decisions you make in the foreground will shape the background.

You paint the background of your life by the accumulated decisions you make in the foreground. Don't live today, totally ignoring what lies a decade hence.

Our Limited Vantage Point

The late humorist Erma Bombeck titled one of her books; *The Grass is Always Greener Over the Septic Tank*. But, if you needed to get a different perspective on things, simply dig down and remove the lid on the septic tank. The stench of reality would cause you to forget the green grass quickly.

Lot focused on the green grass of well-watered plains. Did that single factor alone determine Lot's decision? Were "fat sheep" more important than a healthy family?

Men can fixate on the present. To avoid doing so, you must think long-term. How will this short-term decision affect my children in decades to come? How will it affect your wife? Will your integrity be impacted? More importantly, what about the spiritual implications, not only for you but also for those closest to you?

Wise decision-makers investigate the distance. You make better decisions when you also look to the horizon. Perhaps the idealized "well-watered plains" are not the best choice. Sodom does loom in the distance. Lot's neglect in taking the long look resulted in multiple layers of loss.

Think About It!

1. When they leave home, will my children know how to pray? Will I have been intentional in praying with them and training them to pray? Do they consistently hear me pray?
2. Will my kids know how to find answers to life's dilemmas because they have seen me study and apply the Word?
3. Will my children understand the value of working hard because I went to work every day to provide for their needs?
4. Will my sons and daughters love and esteem their spouse because of my example of loving and honoring their mother?

Chapter 8
Eclipsed Opportunities

A solar eclipse happens when the moon comes between the earth and the sun. On August 21, 2017, in most of North America, the moon obscured the sun. A comparatively small thing eclipsed something massive.

You can create an eclipse. Go outside and close one eye. While looking toward the sun, take a nickel, and gradually move it near your open eye. Soon the sun is obscured.

The insignificant can eclipse the important.

An eclipse of **kindness** happens if you don't consider others in the decisions you make.

> An eclipse of **commitment** occurs if an insignificant hobby becomes your god.

>> An eclipse of **godliness** happens when pleasure comes between you and Jesus.

>>> An eclipse of **faith** has happened if a small problem comes between you and the Lord.

What tiny thing, the proverbial "nickel" has obscured Jesus from your life?

Talent and Opportunity Eclipsed

Two young men from northeast Missouri were born into difficult circumstances. Their mother was addicted to drugs, and their dad was long since absent. Like Sim, the two boys bounced from one foster home to another. Inconsistency and uncertainty were their only constants.

Then the break of a lifetime came. Macon and Louis' final set of foster parents were professionals who provided a stable home. When this family fostered them, Macon and Louis were near adolescence. Things got even better when this family adopted the two boys.

Both boys were talented athletes. When Macon, the older brother, entered high school, college coaches began paying attention. The young man's speed, strength, and talent on the football field and basketball court were spectacular.

When Macon was a junior in high school, the full-fledged recruitment of the young athlete was in full swing. Most days, he received several e-mails from various universities. The best football programs in America offered scholarships.

Macon had been granted an unexpected opportunity. He and Louis lived in a beautiful subdivision with a stable family. Macon's biological mother had cleaned up her act and was again part of her sons' lives. As a high-school senior, Macon was considered the top high school football player in America. On the field, Macon was a man among boys. The school's football and basketball teams both won state championships, with Macon being all-state in both sports. In football, he was the state's Mr. Football.

Macon chose to attend the University of Nebraska. His family was not far away. Historically, Nebraska has been one of America's top football programs. Many Nebraska Cornhusker football players have gone on to play in the National Football League. Macon and the University of Nebraska were a perfect match.

From his first day on campus, Mason was marked. Anyone with a slight interest in football knew who Macon was. Macon lifted weights and worked on drills. He had a goal in mind.

Macon played in every game his freshman year. But at the start of the season the coach did not start Macon. Having started every game during high school, not being the "starter" stung Macon. He didn't like not starting, so Macon redoubled his efforts. By the fourth game, Macon was the starting wide receiver.

Not as many footballs were thrown to him as he'd hoped. Nebraska had a top-line running back. The ball was handed off to that running back 25-30 times each game. Not being the go-to-guy was also new for Macon. He had always been the center of attention on the football field. Now, Macon was an afterthought. Plays designed for his skills were a second or third option.

As might be expected, several girls pursued Macon. Soon he had a steady girlfriend. They were far too intimate. Macon was insecure in relationships. When Macon saw a guy speak to his girlfriend, he would accuse her of not being "faithful." On one such occasion, Macon lost it. He slapped her, leaving her hurt and stunned. Crying, she ran to her apartment and locked the door. Macon beat on her door until security came. He received a citation. When the coach learned of it, he suspended Macon for the next game.

Two weeks later, a policeman stopped Macon for driving erratically. The cop smelled marijuana and asked permission to search Macon's car. The officer found a small bag of pot and arrested Macon. His coach suspended him for the rest of the season. At the same time, the Nebraska head coach made it clear. He wanted Macon to play football for the Nebraska Cornhuskers.

During the following summer, Macon got into a heated argument with another girlfriend. He slapped her and then pushed her down a flight of stairs. The fall broke her wrist. In the Emergency Room, the story came out, resulting in Macon's arrest for domestic violence. An allegation of domestic violence is severe enough to cast a university in a bad light. Nebraska's coach dismissed Macon from the team. If he were to play college football again, it would be at a different university.

Macon's talent and potential were known nationwide, so the University of Texas offered him a scholarship. Under the transfer rules of the National Collegiate Athletic Association (NCAA), Macon could not play for a year. During the year he could not play, Macon hung around the team, worked out, and stayed fit. But by the end of the year, Macon had decided to leave college and make himself available for the National Football League. The New York Giants drafted Macon in the second round, and he received a hefty contract to play four years of professional football.

Macon, now twenty years old, had more money than he'd ever known. The team that drafted him was on America's big stage. New York was far different than any city where Macon had lived. In New York, Macon partied hard. He became known as a playboy, not serious about excelling as an athlete. The Giants kept him on their roster for part of two seasons, then traded him to the Seattle Seahawks. Macon lasted less than a year in Seattle. He seldom played in a game.

On one of Macon's visits home, he got arrested for driving under the influence. The prosecutor cut him a deal. With community service, Macon escaped having a "DUI" on his record. When Seattle removed Macon from their team, not even the worst team in the league wanted him.

Back home, with money still in his pocket, Macon consistently smoked marijuana. He was arrested twice for possession. Then he was caught with more pot than one man could ever use. Found guilty of possession with intent to distribute, the judge sentenced Macon to serve 90 days of a two-year suspended sentence.

Macon was granted a grand opportunity. He had a unique athletic ability. More critical, Mason had people who cared about him, but the young man wasted his chance.

Mason's nickel of selfishness, lack of self-control, and absence of focus eclipsed the blazing sun of his opportunity. What could have been a football career that put Mason in the Hall of Fame, was a failure. Instead of Mason's name in the newspaper for a touchdown scored, it was there to report his felony conviction. Another eclipsed opportunity. You probably know someone who has done the same

Lot's Eclipse

Macon and Lot are similar. Lot knew his uncle was involved in a God-thing. Lot saw it first-hand. But, Lot is only a minor note in history. A footnote of wasted opportunity.

Lot and Macon:

1. Lacked personal discipline.
2. Had mentors who opened the door to great things.
3. Became like errant fireworks fizzling and sparking, but not leaving the ground.

Having a Different Outcome

Recognizing Lot's wrong choices is one thing, but learning from them is another. Applying three truths will make a difference.

<u>Ability will take you only so far</u>. Lot was talented at knowing where to find good grass. He was also good at creating wealth. But, Lot failed to recognize the longterm outcomes that would result from his decisions.

<u>Being unbalanced is dangerous.</u> Lot should have given more thought to protecting his children and partnering with his wife. Lot's life was as out of balance as a two-legged stool. He was interested in success. Lot had no place for God, and his family seems to have been unimportant.

<u>Stay close to your mentor.</u> Mentors accelerate progress. They also help us when they sound a note of warning by saying, "You need to rethink that." Some men seem to want all the voices in their life to be that of a cheerleader instead of a coach! A good coach cheers for you, but he also "kicks your backside" when needed. Too many men don't have, or want, a "kick your backside" mentor.

Think About It!

1. What relatively insignificant things have you seen to create a spiritual eclipse in someone's life?

2. How can a man be sure to keep the small things from getting in the way of the big things?
3. How often do you pause to reset your priorities? Men become unfocused and we must reset. Some time-management gurus recommend doing this quarterly, others say monthly. How do you refocus to make to keep the "main thing the main thing?"

Chapter 9
Settling for Mediocrity

Young men often imagine themselves as a master electrician, diesel mechanic, doctor, attorney, evangelist, or missionary. There is no reason it could not happen. The young visionaries are gifted, capable, and intelligent. Then life happens.

Marriage, a child is born, college is deemed too expensive, credit card debt occurs, or family issues arise.

When such happens, young visionaries "temporarily" settle, thinking, "In a while, life will improve. The journey to my dream can be resumed." Unless a man is persistent, focused, and disciplined, life's complexities will sink the ship of his dreams. The temporary delay becomes permanent.

What did Lot think when Abram *took* him onward? Why did Lot need coercion? Together, the men left Haran in pursuit of spiritual things. Did Lot tire of dusty days and cold nights? Whatever the reason, Lot no longer wanted to participate. Abram talked about God's promise for the future. Lot, however, was more interested in the "present land" than the "promised land."

The Influence of "Stuff"

Men are easily distracted, and Satan specializes in distraction. In Mark 4, Jesus talked about the seed of His Word and spoke of "thorny ground." The seed sown on the thorny ground was unaffected by birds, the heat, or rocks. The sole problem was other things that co-existed in the field. The other stuff took vital energy, so the plant lived, though it was never productive. (Mark 4:7)

Jesus described the "other things" the thorns:

> Cares of this world
>> Deceitfulness of riches
>>> The lust for other things. (Mark 4:19)

The "other things" don't necessarily make a *sin list*. "Other things" like hunting, golf, knife collecting, soccer, the stock market, music, or following baseball are not naturally wrong. Paul often used athletic terms. He knew about running races, wrestling, and obtaining the prize. David fought a bear and a lion. Christian men retain their competitiveness and drive.

It is when those "other things" drain your spiritual vitality that productivity is choked. Men can continue to be consistent in church attendance or giving, but not be the soul-winner they had envisioned. A sense of being eager to "do" for God is gone.

A Settler or a Seeker?

Lot settled, while Abram sought. Abram's quest impacted future generations. Abraham was still alive when his grandsons, Jacob and Esau, were young adults. Rabbinical writers say Abraham often talked of being called from Ur and of God's provision for his family. The now aged "seeker" influenced young Jacob. Inspired by his grandfather's stories, Jacob desired both the family birthright and his father's blessing. Abram kept talking about what it was he sought.

Men who "settle" for stuff also talk. Listen, and you soon know whether a man has stopped seeking. We give ourselves away. *"...for, of the abundance of the heart his mouth speaketh,"* (Luke 6:45).

Such a man can tell you more about NASCAR than the pastor's series on *The Benefit of the Holy Ghost*. He knows the lifetime batting average of Babe Ruth but does not know who Paul was. Such men's adventure with God is constrained. They settle for pennies while gold is available. Lot eagerly pursued the mundane, as does any man who lets God's seed be choked with this world's thorns.

Mid-Life Settling

We don't know Lot's exact age when he made these decisions. But, from observation, we know that the middle years of life are dangerous.

On the basketball court, you are the last man picked. In a mid-life crisis, some men settle for a new wife instead of a renewed commitment to marriage. Chamomile tea and warm flannel have replaced the warm fuzzies of candlelit romance; hair is gray or gone; at your abdomen, a keg has replaced the "six-pack:" the primary use of your "guns" is to pick up a remote control.

What drives this mid-life mess? Perhaps the sense that life is quickly passing?

When you see a Christian fellow, closer to geezer age than teenage, sporting around town in a convertible, a tanning salon glow, with a new woman by his side – that man has "settled." What you see is not what God had in mind. But the fellow became weary with the journey. Be wary of your middle-years moments. It is wise to find someone who can be a voice of reason.

As a child, your mom looked over your shoulder to inspect your schoolwork. At university, mom is no longer there. Similarly, when Lot was young, Abram would not permit him to settle. When Lot reached the age of, "I'll do it my way," he settled. He became content with prosperity and being a man of influence in Sodom. Lot's voice was silent toward God. His desire for "other things" had control of the field that was Lot's life. He would never be productive for God.

Think About It!

1. Think back to your late teens and early twenties. What did you dream of accomplishing, inventing, writing, or doing? For most of us, life intrudes on at least some of our hopes and dreams. Can you recall the events that got in the way of you moving forward toward your goal?
2. Abram sought while Lot settled. Abram was something of an experimenter; he did not feel the need to do business as usual. Abram's faith in God made him comfortable with traveling into the unknown. What are some things in God that you'd yet like

to explore? How does a person go about entering into adventuring with God?
3. Pay attention to the thorns in your spiritual life. Every farmer fights weeds. Weeds are his enemy because they stop productivity. The "cares of life, the deceitfulness of riches, and the desire for other things" will disrupt what a man can do for God. Make a listing for "cares of life," then another list for each of the other two. A man needs to identify his thorns.
4. When tempted to settle, don't forget that every man faces the same temptations. As you look in the eyes of a man celebrating his 50th wedding anniversary, or his 20th year of service as a Sunday School teacher know this; that man had opportunities to quit. It takes commitment to pursue the best God has for you.
5. Evaluate your commitment to the following things on a scale of 1-10:

    The Lord Jesus Christ

    Marriage

    Children

    Church

    Career
6. Remember the season of your most significant commitment to God. What brought you to that level of commitment?
7. Perhaps your commitment has wavered at times. What caused that loss?

Chapter 10
Is Prosperity Your Priority?

Joe was a devoted Christian. Godly men influenced him in both the Word and the Spirit. Joe learned well; his knowledge was not just in his head. As a young man, Godly men and his devotion to God guided his decisions. His commitment resulted in Joe eventually becoming a deacon. He was a servant. If there was work to do about the church, Joe was involved. His wife and children were equally active.

With God's good favor, Joe launched a trucking company transporting coal mining equipment. Initially, it was Joe alone, working long hours. He often worked late, but Joe remained steadfast. He was faithful to church. Joe usually looked tired, and there were some events he did not attend.

Then came a booming demand for his trucking service. Joe took advantage of the opportunity. Who wouldn't? More trucks were needed, and Joe bought land for a "truck yard," where he built a mechanics shop. Joe hired drivers, mechanics, roustabouts, and office staff.

He had found a good thing. The money flowed. Soon, Joe's cash flow was millions of dollars each year. Profits exceeded $500,000. The work was demanding. Being "the boss" almost always is. Stress left Joe physically, mentally, emotionally, and spiritually drained. In a simpler time, Joe's day started with prayer and reading his well-marked Bible. Now, Joe's days began in high gear. There was no time for quiet moments with God.

Success should be enjoyed. Joe's family members drove luxury vehicles. Each year the ladies of the family visited the "market" in Dallas to secure current fashions. They lived in a beautiful home on "Snob Hill." In the community, Joe garnered respect. His hard work and entrepreneurial mindset had again proven that a man could succeed.

A boy raised in the backwoods; Joe had never imagined having wealth. Now it was his. People commented about how God had blessed Joe and his family.

When is a Blessing Not a Blessing?

Was it a blessing? It depends on how you measure life.

Joe attempted or said he tried to attend church regularly. But he wasn't there much. He made sure to mail his tithe and offering. Often, several weeks would elapse between Joe's appearances in church. He was busy. There were deals to make, contracts to read, and decisions to make. Besides, Joe needed some time for himself.

The word "busy" identified the entire family. At the trucking company, his wife was second in command. Joe's children – who had once taught Sunday school and sang in the choir – were consumed with company business. Joe's children became even less committed than their father. In time, they no longer attended church.

Joe decided that money mattered a great deal. He sacrificed his spiritual life on the altar of success. Jesus said such would happen. The synoptic gospels warn:

> ...*How hardly shall they that have riches enter into the kingdom of God!* [25] *For it is easier for a camel to go through a needle's eye, than for a rich man to enter into the kingdom of God*, (Luke 18:24-25).

Lot's Great Substance

Lot made a similar decision to Joe. Wealth, prosperity, and success mattered to Lot. After leaving Haran, Abram traveled to Canaan, then on to Egypt. When Abram and his entourage returned to Canaan, they were wealthy.

So much so, that when Lot's name recurs, the Bible points out Lot's prosperity.

And Lot also, which went with Abram, had flocks, and herds, and tents. And the land was not able to bear them, that they might dwell together: for their substance was great,... (Genesis 13:5-6).

Lot had succeeded. He was wealthy.

The Benefit of Simplicity

Low-income families live simple lives. The majority of people in the world live from one payday to the next. If Lot had owned two skinny goats, five sickly sheep, and a leaking tent, life would have been simple. He would have remained in the company of Abram.

If Lot's life had been simple:

- He'd have been there when God changed Abram's name to Abraham.
- He would have known more about Abraham's altars and less about Sodom's perversion.
- Lot's wife might have heard Sarai laugh at hearing angels say the older woman was going to have a baby.
- Lot would have heard the first cries of baby Isaac.

Prosperity and the pursuit of "more" create the crossroads of many decisions.

Money Trouble

Lot's great substance (Genesis 15:6) was not enough. He wanted more. As a rich man, Lot did what a poor man could not have done. He separated from his mentor, Abraham, the "father of the faithful."

Remember Joe and the trucking company? Joe's "great substance" resulted in him losing his intimacy with Jesus. His children backslid and are now cynical about Christianity. Add eternity to the equation, and Joe did not succeed.

All wealth is temporary; there are no rich dead men. Lot's wealth disappeared in the ash of Sodom and Gomorrah. Genesis 13:5

mentions Lot's tents, flocks, and herd, which he had in abundance. But when Lot, his wife, and two younger daughters left Sodom, there was no mention of tents, flocks or herds. Any money Lot had gained in Sodom was forever gone.

In deciding to pursue wealth, Lot chased after that which can not be retained.

Not a Poverty Doctrine

Lot's success was not his problem. How Lot dealt with success was the problem. Joe's many trucks, numerous contracts, and substantial cash-flow were not an issue. What men must address when making decisions is, how will this change my priorities? Joe shifted from godliness to the pursuit of gold. Lot and Joe both made decisions to pursue enormous wealth.

Being concerned about prosperity is not the basis of a "poverty doctrine." Some men have become wealthy and kept their priorities right. Abram had "great substance" and never lost sight of what was important.

What brings you contentment? Are you fully satisfied with the physical? Or do you still yearn for the things of God?

The difference between Abram and Lot:

> Lot's desire for wealth became the motive for his decisions.

> Abram never let money affect his decisions.

For every man who correctly handles wealth, dozens cannot. What Richard Foster called "the kingdom of thingdom," has led to many foolish decisions.

Here are symptoms of misplaced priorities:

- "Work" consistently keeps you away from corporate prayer meetings and church.
- The tithe of your increase would be so much money that you finagle a way to receive a minimal "salary." You then tithe on a

relatively small amount of money, while your wholly-owned corporation makes millions.

- There is no longer time to serve. NO time exists to be an usher, teacher, Home Bible Study teacher, or to help with disciple-making.

When men have misplaced priorities, God and family get the leftovers of their time, energy, and ability.

The Proper Use of Prosperity

No, success is not a "dirty word." Men are encouraged to improve their situation. Do well for your family. If God blesses you with wealth, bless His work abundantly. Do as King David. Since God would not let David build a temple, he did the next best thing by using his wealth to generously prepare for the eventual building of the temple (1 Chronicles 22:1-5).

In the New Testament, Barnabas sold property and gave the proceeds to advance Jesus' work (Acts 4:36-37). Lydia, a business owner in Thyatira, provided her home as the location from which Paul, Silas, and Timothy evangelized Thyatira (Acts 16:15). These people exemplify how prosperity can bless God's work.

God <u>never</u> blesses a man for him to be a miser. If God blesses you with millions, provide hundreds of thousands to His work. If God blesses you with billions, provide tens of millions to His work. Give liberally. There are churches to build, evangelistic campaigns to accomplish, and missions work to establish.

Think About It!

1. Be careful what you pursue. *"What does it profit a man if he gains the whole world and loses his soul?"* (Matthew 16:26; Mark 8:36). Ask God never to let you become prosperous if prosperity causes you, your wife, and children to be lost.

2. Know the source of your "great abundance." Yes, your diligence is to be honored. But you could be physically, mentally, or emotionally impaired to the point where you could accomplish

nothing. Always acknowledge the Lord Jesus Christ as having granted you the opportunity to succeed. Your honor to Him should include giving liberally.

3. Submit your career or entrepreneurial success to your pastor and another Godly man. Invite them to challenge your priorities if they see you slip. You won't like it when they challenge you, but when they do, recognize their love for you.

4. As God blesses you, don't base what you give on what others can contribute. Some could provide $100,000 or $1,000,000 to advance God's work. Unfortunately, some who could do so are satisfied to give $15,000. They are comfortable with this because they know the most anyone else in the church can bring is $5,000. Contribute based on how God has blessed you. Never compare your giving to others. Be blind to what others can or cannot do.

Chapter 11
Yesterday's Memories

Ur, the city Abram and Lot left was a relatively modern city having a quality of life some third world cities do not now enjoy. Ur had hot and cold running water, a sewer system, multistory buildings, paved roads, and ornate furniture. The Sumerians, the primary culture group in Ur, were inventive. These were the people who divided the hour into 60 minutes, a minute into 60 seconds, and the circle into 360 degrees.

Ur's canals connected the Tigris and Euphrates rivers; these controlled floods and irrigated crops. Because of irrigation, farming went on year-round. Life in Ur was good.

The Danger of Selective Memory

This urban "good life" had been Lot's home. Later in life, Sodom was the nearest thing to Ur that was available. Cities like Ur and Sodom had cultural benefits. It had a thriving market, and stimulating conversation and wealth quickly established influence.

As is typical for all, Lot's memories of youth would have been selective. My memories of Junior High include making the end-of-the-game free throw to win a sixth-grade intramural basketball tournament. I didn't make all my free-throws, but I don't remember any misses. Meanwhile, half of a century later, that specific free throw is well-remembered.

It's called selective memory! My college memories include a professor saying, "Carlton, your writing has great potential." My college GPA shows other professors were not as favorable. I don't recall what any of them said about my work. It's selective memory at work.

Did Lot choose to remember the *good* of city-life and ignore the bad? Selective memory can cause men to return to a life of which they repented. Selective memory:

- The man smiling with pleasure while telling of the booze-laden parties is forgetting throwing up in his friend's new car.
- Remembers the "buzz," but forgets the humiliation of being arrested for "Driving Under the Influence." Forgets how he felt when someone forwarded him his picture from Mugshots.com.
- Recalls the allure of sexual adventure but forgets the fear and humiliation of being tested for a sexually transmitted disease.
- Remembers the thousands of dollars picked up in one night of poker while forgetting that most nights he went bust, leaving too little money to buy groceries.

At the behest of an invisible deity not usually worshipped in Ur, Abram had left comfort and luxury. Ur, or anything like it, no longer attracted Abram. Something better awaited Abram.

Did Lot remember Ur while at the same time ignoring all he had learned about God?

Return Trips

Selective memory is dangerous, causing a man to seek "what used to be." Ur's dry climate with sunny days may appeal if the comparison is dusty days of travel followed by cold nights. Recalling running water as you go days with no fresh water will make you long for the "good old days."

If Lot's memories moved him to seek a city like Ur, he was letting yesterday's imperfect memory affect today's decision. He was also ignoring the impact of today's decisions on tomorrow.

Are your recent decisions positioning your wife and children for a better tomorrow? Lot's choices did not.

Comfort or Commitment?

God's promise does not assure ease. It didn't work that way for Abraham, Isaac, Jacob, or Paul. Why would you be the exception?

Some sinful men have made vast sums of money by taking advantage of others. Then Jesus saves them and gives them a different lifestyle. Poker tables and casinos are no longer comfortable for the former gambler. The shady businessman decides to have integrity in his dealings.

If men are doing the will of God, won't their lives be more comfortable? Won't such men immediately flourish? Perhaps, or perhaps not.

Abram became wealthy and established a nation, but he never found that for which he sought, (Hebrews 11:9-10). For centuries to come, Canaan was not a luxurious place to live. The terrain was rugged, the climate was harsh, and inconsistent water supplies often produced drought and famine. Life was never as easy as it was back in Ur.

So, did God fail Abram? Wasn't Lot wise to try to make the best of what seemed to be a bad situation?

Again, the comparison is wrong. A commitment to Godly living is not a commitment to comfort; instead, it is a commitment to making right choices. To the Christians of the first century, Paul wrote:

> ...*come out from among them, and **be ye separate**, saith the Lord, and touch not the unclean thing; and I will receive you*, (2 Corinthians 6:17).

Modern hucksters marketing Christianity without change are lying. Easy-believism is like a knock-off cologne. Both lose their scent and significance. God's men are called to simplicity of life, modesty, and distinctiveness from the world. It is a commitment to God's way and will.

Contentment is a Decision

If a Godly man chooses not to go to the pub "with the boss and the boys," could he be overlooked for a promotion? It happens. Other men work in highly competitive areas selling equipment worth millions of dollars. Some salesmen grease the wheels. They don't give the purchasing agent a kickback. That would be illegal. But what can it hurt to have a case of fine Scotch Whiskey delivered to the purchasing agent's home? If a Godly man refuses to do such things, will he lose sales? He may! The decision to do what was right has cost more than one man a job.

How should a man respond to inequity and disappointment? Paul wrote,

> *In whatsoever state I'm in, therewith to be content. I know both how to be abased, and I know how to abound…,* (Philippians 4: 11b-12a).

Paul <u>decided</u> to be content. Contentment is a choice. Some who leave the gaming tables, nightclubs, and unethical lifestyle for the things of God, eventually become discontented. The old way now seems better. Such men can make foolish decisions, endangering himself, his family, and others.

As Lot gazed longingly toward the well-watered plains and significant cities of Sodom and Gomorrah, did they remind him of Ur? From all appearances, Sodom and Gomorrah seemed better than Canaan, so when the opportunity came, Lot pitched his tent toward Sodom.

The Temptation to Return

The temptation to return to the old may be driven by current difficulty or a well-sanitized memory of how life "used to be."

- Israel escaped being slaves to the Egyptians, but at times they wanted to return, (Exodus 16:2-3; 17:1-3; Numbers 11:4-5; 14:1-35).
- Early in a missionary effort, John Mark left the work of missions, (Acts 15:36-39).
- Those who followed Jesus for miracles, returned home when He began talking of difficulties to come. He even asked the apostles, "Wilt thou also go away? (John 6:66-69).

Simon Peter used vivid imagery to describe those who return to old things.

[20]For if after they have escaped the pollutions of the world through the knowledge of the Lord and Saviour Jesus Christ, they are again entangled

therein, and overcome, the latter end is worse with them than the beginning. ²¹For it had been better for them not to have known the way of righteousness, than, after they have known it, to turn from the holy commandment delivered unto them. <u>²²But it is happened unto them according to the true proverb, The dog is turned to his own vomit again; and the sow that was washed to her wallowing in the mire,</u> (2 Peter 2:20-22).

Don't be entangled in the old life. Don't recall that old life through rose-colored glasses.

Think About It

1. What do you most miss about your "pre-Christ" life? Hopefully, unrealistic memories are not tugging at you. Stop and think about the negative consequences of your past behavior. Was there the potential for a sexually transmitted disease? Could those actions have resulted in you getting a DWI or becoming an addict? Were you spending money you did not have to gamble or support a habit that you hid from your wife?

2. When you add Jesus' promises into your decision-making process, does your "old life" compare with what lies before you? What can you do to keep from being enticed back to the past life?

3. Contentment is a decision. In what area do you find yourself tending toward being discontented? This area of life will need vigilant protection. Healthy men decide to be content with what will always be an imperfect life.

Chapter 12
Direction Determines Destination

Abram was a fan of the Almighty. To use a sports analogy, Abram had all the God-gear. As a fan, he wore the sweatshirt, had a pennant, a bumper sticker, cap, necktie, and winter coat. If you were around Abram very long, you knew what he believed.

Abram or Lot

- Abram would have blessed any local church. Lot would have watched the local church – if that.
- Abram would have attended every prayer meeting. Lot would not have known the church had prayer meetings.
- Abram would have been the first to give sacrificially. Lot would have given grudgingly, if he gave at all.
- Abram was dedicated to God. Lot was committed to…well, Lot was committed to Lot.

Would other people say you were more like Abram or like Lot? How do you see yourself – as a Lot or Abram?

When Paths Separate

The two men who had shared much were oh, so different. Lot applied different values. The lack of the Lord's influence on Lot is evident.

While Abraham had at least thirteen personal encounters with God.

> Lot had none.

While, Abraham built four altars to God.

> Lot built none.

Lot could tell stories about God.

> But Lot had no commitment to the God of the stories.

After Lot's Look

Lot beheld, chose, and journeyed.

> ...and Lot dwelled in the cities of the plain, and pitched his tent toward Sodom, (Genesis 13:12)

The Torah used the verb "va'ye'ehal." It translates, "and Lot tented *toward* Sodom." The term, "tented toward" is an unusual way to speak of a man's residence.

The Torah generally used one of two other words to speak of a residence. One word indicated a home in a specific location, a permanent residence. The second word, often translated, *to dwell*, showed a temporary residence.

Genesis 13:12 uses an even more transient term. An example of the distinction between the two phrases would be:

- *"To dwell"* would refer to renting a house for a year of college.
- *"Tenting"* would speak of setting up a tent for a week of camping.

Lot "tented toward Sodom." There was nothing permanent about his first stop on the Jordanian plains. Lot set up his tents in a way that made it easy to move on.

Another word has significance. The KJV translates the word as *toward*. In other translations of Hebrew writing, this word is often translated *"until."* It was a concept of uncertainty. Concerning both distance and time, the word *"until"* lacks certainty. Examples of such uses of *"until "* may help:

- In giving directions, someone says, "Travel south *until* you see the red barn, then turn west." How far is it to the red barn? Who knows? The word *"until"* does not specify.
- Another man explaining his family's living situation said, "We will live here *until* something better comes along." How long will it be *until* something better arrives? The word *"until"* does not stipulate.

Lot tented, *ad Sodom*, (in English it would translate, "*until* Sodom"). Lot's situation is unclear. Was Lot in Sodom or just outside? There is uncertainty. Perhaps Lot was halting between two opinions? (1 Kings 18:21) More likely, "until Sodom" meant Lot tented at that location, until he became comfortable with Sodom being his home.

A reason to be uncertain is seen in the next sentence: *"But the men of Sodom were wicked and sinners before the LORD exceedingly,"* (Genesis 13:13). Lot was not ignorant of the nature of Sodom.

Lot knew but yet decided to tent *until* Sodom. He moved his family close. Indecisiveness was part of Lot's character. Did Lot imagine he could live *toward* Sodom, and it not affect his family? Or was he just waiting to be comfortable with the wickedness of Sodom.

The Danger of Wanting Too Much

It was a slippery slope because Lot desired some things Sodom had. His tent door opened toward Sodom. A man edging away from God is not planning to abandon Jesus. Instead, he wants Jesus ***and*** something else. The *something else* is that man's Sodom.

Jesus taught, *"No man can serve two masters,"* (Matthew 6:24). Elijah challenged the Hebrews, who tried serving two different gods. *"How long halt ye between two opinions? If the Lord be God, follow him: but if Baal, then follow him"* (1 Kings 18:21). You cannot have it both ways.

Can any love the Lord with heart, soul, mind, and strength, and at the same time, value their version of "Sodom"?

Lot's thinking was flawed.

- Sodom was near.
- Sodom was wicked.
- Sodom was ungodly.
- Sodom was immoral.

Yet, Lot's behavior said, "I want Sodom." Lot reached the time and place where his "*until*" was fulfilled. To reuse the earlier word-pictures, Lot came to the red barn, and he felt something better had arrived. With that, Lot turned toward Sodom and moved in.

Rejecting Sodom's Influence

How can you keep from the same outcome? Instead, of "tenting toward" Sodom, erect barriers against Sodom.

- Be mindful of the "Jesus and _____" times of your life. These can slip up on you. Compromises of morals, ethics, and integrity are common when a man wants Jesus and _____.

- Guard your home. Put parental controls on the technology your children use – even into adolescence. Slowly loosen the restrictions, only after giving clear guidance on how to use the device.

- Intentionally, introduce your family to the concept of a Biblical worldview. Seriously equip them as to what a Biblical worldview entails. You want your children to view life differently than other kids.

- If possible, take the lead, and make the sacrifices to involve your children in Bible quizzing or some other form of focused Bible understanding.

- Communicate to your family that legalization or normalization does not mean specific actions are no longer sin. Imbibing alcohol, smoking marijuana, cohabiting, and same-sex relationships will always be wrong in God's sight.

- If homeschooling fits your family dynamic, make use of these resources. A quality Christian school can also be an option. In America, some states offer online options to homeschool.

- Stay involved in your child's life. It is, at times, inconvenient, but much safer for the neighborhood teens to gather at your home than for your teens to be elsewhere.

- When you learn that their education involves something anti-Biblical, speak up. Don't pander to the media, but express your concern to the teacher and then to school administration.

Think About It

1. What you bring your family "toward" will impact them. What you move them "away" from also matters. Lot not only moved toward wicked Sodom, but he also moved away from Godly Abram. Do your decisions move your family closer to the people of God, or Sodom?
2. Your decisions are more important than the things you say. You tell your son, "Say that word again, and I'll wash your mouth out with soap." Meanwhile, your family is being entertained by television, movies, books, and magazines using those same words. You are "tenting toward" Sodom. How long before you abandon any pretense of godliness?
3. As in Sodom, homosexuality and graphic violence are normalized in modern video games. Video game manufacturers dub their best gamers as "gods." Are you endorsing your children's fall into idolatry by allowing them to become "gamer gods and goddesses"? Are you creating difficulties for your children to serve Jesus by introducing them to the world's modern version of Sodom?

Sodom

Chapter 13
Consider Your Risks

Between Genesis 13:14 and 14:12, Lot chose the well-watered plains of the Jordan River. He subsequently pitched his family's tent toward Sodom. By Genesis 14:12, Lot is living in Sodom.

While Lot settled in Sodom, Abram had another God encounter:

- *And the LORD said unto Abram… Lift up now thine eyes,…. For all the land which thou seest, to thee will I give it, and to thy seed…,* (Genesis 13:14-15).
- *And I will make thy seed as the dust of the earth…,* (Genesis 13:16).
- *Walk through the land…for I will give it unto thee.* (Genesis 13:17).

Abram's experience was compelling. God described a glorious future. At the same time, Abram was also making some decisions.

- Abram relocated to Hebron, which further distanced him from Sodom. (Genesis 13:18)
- Abram decided to build an altar to God. (Genesis 13:18)

When he moved in, Lot may not have noticed that the city of Sodom was subject to Chedorlaomer, the king of Elam. (Genesis 14:1-7) The relationship between Elam and Sodom would have been like nations in the British Empire. A few decades ago, Britain controlled India, America, Australia, and other countries. Much of the wealth of those nations flowed to Britain.

The king of Elam taxed Sodom. Sodom was subject to the authority of Chedorlaomer, the king of Elam.

Easy Bondage

Lot's move into Sodom took his family to a city controlled by a foreign king. Lot chose the loose bondage of Sodom over the liberty of the mountains to the west. Lot preferred being an "upscale slave" in a setting that pleased his physical senses, ambitions, and ego rather than a free man with a hard life. Sodom seemed to suit Lot, even as Sodom put Lot at risk.

Comfortable bondage is still a "thing." Chains covered with velvet hold a man just as tightly as does naked steel. Satan employs easy bondage. Men controlled without their even realizing it sense no danger, pain, or loss. Men allow themselves to be locked in velvet chains for one of two reasons:

1. The chains appeal to their human appetites.
2. Chains provide certainty, while faith involves uncertainty.

After years of being vassals to Chedorlaomer, the king of Sodom and several kings in the same situation rebelled, (Genesis 14:1-7). Chedorlaomer defeated Sodom and Gomorrah. (Genesis 14:8-10).

The conquering king took away the valuables of Sodom. Often, such conquerors would also carry away the people considered to be the wealthiest or elite of the city. Such captives were held for ransom, became slaves, or were displayed as trophies. For one of these purposes, Chedorlaomer took Lot captive (Genesis 14:11-12).

Choosing Sodom? Expect the Unexpected

Lot never planned to live in Elam. Certainly not as a slave to Chedorlaomer. Elam was a distant city of which Lot likely knew little. Did Lot realize life in Sodom put him at risk of slavery? Or had the leaders of Sodom hidden all visible reminders that the king of Elam was lord of their city? Did Lot ask questions about to whom he would pay his taxes and who governed Sodom?

The Risk of Sodom

Choosing a course that ignores God is dangerous. Bad decisions lead to subtle bondage. The task-master seems easy, and the "velvet chains" are never tight. But what starts pleasant ends ugly. Lot is not the only example.

- Samson was a "he-man with a she problem." From Samson's youth, seeing a pretty Philistine girl caused him to take a second look. What hurt could there be in a marriage or perhaps even a dalliance with a cute Philistine girl? Later, when Samson, now blinded, was turning the Philistines' mill, we could ask him, "Samson, was it worth the risk?"

- King Saul gradually departed from humility and obedience to God. He impatiently stepped beyond his responsibilities into those of priest and prophet. He died a loser. Saul, "Was it worth the risk?"
- Gehazi, the prophet Elisha's servant, sought personal gain from the now healed Naaman. It seemed so innocent. Later, as Gehazi's body was being devoured by leprosy, ask him, "Was it worth the risk?"

Comfortable bondage is so prevalent. The natural curiosity to know more about sexual things could have been awakened in a youngster, but in time the natural curiosity becomes obsessive. The feelings are pleasant, and besides, "everybody is doing it." But the "velvet chains" of sexual addiction are being locked tightly about that man. Just like Lot moved into Sodom, perhaps without knowing there was another ruler, that man is eventually dominated by a continual pursuit of pornography. A healthy marital relationship is unlikely. Ask him, "Was it worth the risk?"

Men have succumbed to the comfortable bondage of gambling, only to lose their business. "Was it worth the risk?"

Another comes under the sway of methamphetamine to provide more energy. He can work longer and harder and get more done. Then he needs the rush. Soon his body is ruined. "Was it worth the risk?"

"Velvet chains," you have seen them: cocaine, alcohol, the "other woman," money, success, and power all have controlled men.

Life is full of unknowns; just as being taken captive by Chedorlaomer was something Lot did not anticipate. But Lot had put himself in a dangerous place.

The Faith Option

When life's unknowns come, is it not best to address them from a place of faith rather than from comfortable bondage?

Often when the unknown and unanticipated comes, things like disease, an addicted child, the potential for a prison term, job loss, parental woes, or marital chaos, those in "easy bondage" wish for faith. But the life of faith was left on the mountain with Uncle Abram. Instead, they chose the risky life of Sodom.

Think About It!

1. What did Lot risk losing when he moved into Sodom? Why was there a risk associated with the well-watered plains? Do you suppose the well-watered plains had little danger if Lot had remained outside Sodom? When we begin to accept small risks, are we soon willing to take on a more significant risk?
2. What do you see as three high-risk decisions a man can make regarding his spiritual condition?
3. What are the more risky things from which a man needs to protect his family? How do you suggest he provide that protection?

Chapter 14
Second Chances

And it came to pass in the days of Amraphel king of Shinar, Arioch king of Ellasar, Chedorlaomer king of Elam, and Tidal king of nations; ²That these made war with Bera king of Sodom, and with Birsha king of Gomorrah, . . . ⁸And there went out the king of Sodom, and the king of Gomorrah, . . . and they joined battle with them in the vale of Siddim; ¹⁰And the vale of Siddim was full of slimepits; and the kings of Sodom and Gomorrah fled, and fell there; . . . . ¹¹And they took all the goods of Sodom and Gomorrah, . . . ¹²And they took Lot, ¹³And there came one that had escaped, and told Abram the Hebrew . . . ¹⁴And when Abram heard . . . he armed his trained servants, . . . And he brought back all the goods, and . . . Lot . . . . (Genesis 14:1-16)

Abram chose to rescue Lot. Despite the odds being against Abram and his servants, they prevailed against forces led by three kings. God was at work. Abram rescued Lot and restored what had been taken from Sodom and Gomorrah.

After the battle, Sodom's king came to meet Abram. He was appreciative and encouraged Abram to keep the recovered goods (Genesis 14:20-24).

Abram's response was abrupt, *"I will not take from a thread even to a shoelatchet, . . ., lest thou shouldest say, I have made Abram rich,"* (Genesis 14:23). Abram did not want any association with Sodom.

Lot, had now been rescued from bondage by Abram, a man of faith.

Lot moved right back into the setting that had resulted in his capture.

For a second time, Lot decided to call Sodom home!

Did Lot being rescued result in anything positive? Seemingly not. Lot's descendants vexed Israel for centuries. Does it not seem that these events would have allowed Lot to rethink his decision to make Sodom his home? If his capture and rescue offered an opportunity to escape, Lot chose to ignore it. He returned to his address in Sodom.

Rescued – to What End

Sven was a man with significant health issues. He was significantly less committed to Jesus than sports. When, in addition to several other health problems, Sven's liver began to fail, he became more serious about God. Prayer and church attendance grew important.

Miraculously, a liver became available for Sven. Soon he was physically better, but Sven's spiritual condition got worse. He refused to participate in any spiritual discipline. His arrogance and narcissism could be seen from 100 yards away. A life-threatening health crisis was averted, but to what end?

Abram's courageous rescue of Lot presents the same question: to what end?

Lot's Folly

Lot had become comfortable. He chose to be blind to Sodom's dangers. Lot either could not or would not admit that moving to Sodom was a mistake. Stubbornness, like that shown in Lot, has destroyed many. Stubborn men make stupid decisions!

Lot was like a man driving across the American southwest who said, "I took a wrong turn thirty miles back, but surely somewhere ahead, there will be a shortcut across the desert." He continued driving until the fuel tank was dry. That man died trying to walk to safety. Bad decisions are part of life. But at times, you need to turn around and start over. Lot was not wise.

If you have made bad choices and been rescued, don't be so unwise. Jesus has extended His mercy and grace to you. Those who have invested in you have not abandoned you. These men stand ready to assist in your recovery. Leave behind your earlier lousy decision and move away from your Sodom. Do it now! It is a necessary step of repentance.

Think About It!

1. Can you think of a decision you made and later wished you had the opportunity for a "re-do?"
2. What do you think causes men to be so stubborn? Why do we hold to bad decisions even when we realize things are not going well?
3. Put yourself in Lot's shoes. You have decided to live in Sodom. Subsequently, a foreign king has captured you. Then you were rescued by someone who loves you like a brother. How would you respond toward Abram? How would you feel about the choice you had made, and what would you change after the experience of having been taken captive and rescued?

Chapter 15
Lack of Gratitude

Some decisions are unconscious. We act without thought. Having driven for years, the automatic habits of starting the vehicle's engine, putting the car in gear, and then steering requires no conscious thought. But each action the driver took needed a decision.

You are also unconsciously restrained from doing certain things. These unconscious restraints can be good or bad.

- You may not even think about entering a nightclub. As an adult, you have every right to enter. But, unconsciously, you have made a decision.
- Failing to recall your wedding anniversary, your wife's birthday, or being consistently disrespectful can also be unconscious.

But, you can make yourself conscious of both good and bad conduct. With work, you can overcome lousy behavior.

Your wedding anniversary, essential birthdays, etc. can be put on your calendar. A smartphone app or computer program can be set to remind you of important dates.

Unconscious actions become grooves worn in the pavement of life. Like all of us, Lot made unconscious decisions. His attitude of disrespect seemed to be habitual and Lot had at least one more bad habit.

After Abram's Victory

Abram had involved himself in Sodom's troubles for one reason. (Genesis 14:21-23) His nephew Lot was in trouble.

The king of Sodom publicly expressed his gratitude for Abram's intervention. Many things were wrong in Sodom, but the king of Sodom sounded the right note of appreciation.

A Missing "Thank You"

Who never spoke a word of gratitude? Lot! The heathen king of a godless, immoral city said, "Thank you" while Lot said nothing.

Did Lot not understand the significance of being rescued? That seems unlikely. Would not Lot have been grateful for Abram's help? Perhaps Lot was incapable of expressing his appreciation.

- When Abram and Lot separated, Lot was allowed the first choice of where to settle, (Genesis 13:7-11). Was Lot appreciative? If so, the Bible does not record it.
- Delivered from the king of Sodom by Abram's intervention, Lot never said, "Thank you."
- When angels warned Lot of impending destruction and led him from Sodom, Lot did not tell them, "Thank you."

Like many men, Lot never thought to be thankful.

Be Thankful!

If you habitually do not express appreciation, retrain yourself. Several steps can help to create a habit of thankfulness.

1. Realize the importance of not taking any blessing or benefit for granted. You have much for which to be thankful.
2. Intentionally <u>express your appreciation</u>. Unexpressed thanks are perceived as meaning you are not appreciative.
3. Be mindful of life's movement around you. Keep a *Gratitude Journal*. At the end of each day, you write down those things for which you are thankful. The list should be specific.
4. Based on your *Gratitude Journal* express, "Thanks" to those who help you. Phrases we don't use become ever harder to put to use. Conversely, when you begin to say, "Thank you," it becomes easier to repeat it.

Lot not only never said, "Thank you" to Abram; he also didn't say, "Thank you" when God later delivered him from Sodom.

> Those who do not say, "Thanks," to people,
> Seldom say, "Thanks" to God!

Perilously Unthankful

Thankfulness is important. Being unappreciative is a sign of the last days. Unthankful people often have a sense of privilege. A sense of entitlement is the opposite to living by grace. Paul wrote:

> *This know also, that in the last days, perilous times shall come for men shall be... unthankful...,"* (2 Timothy 3:1-2).

Verses 2-5 list some traits of the last days:

lovers of self	covetous (envious)
boasters	proud
blasphemers (irreverent of sacred things)	disobedient to parents
unthankful	unholy
Without natural affection (untrustworthy)	trucebreakers
false accusers	incontinent
fierce	despisers of those that are good
traitors	heady (headstrong)
highminded (arrogant)	pleasure-loving
professing godliness with no power	

This list does not result from perilous times. The "hard" times come because of these behaviors. *Unthankfulness* is part of creating a climate of peril. The word translated *perilous* in the KJV means, "reduced strength, difficult, or dangerous." Unthankful men make for weak, difficult, and dangerous times. Unthankful men produce a weak nation, derelict churches, and sad families.

Is entitlement part of the way you think? I'm entitled to…? It is my right…? Who writes a "thank you" note to their government, or a neighboring taxpayer, for health care, welfare, a free cell phone, free higher education or subsidized housing? Instead, many people feel they rightfully deserve such things at no cost. Entitled men take their blessings for granted. They only speak up if something is at risk of being taken away.

Did Lot even see good things for what they were? Lot's family was wealthy, and personal success came his way. Did Lot assume he deserved the good coming his way? To the point that he was never thankful?

Filling Your Gratitude Journal

Unthankful men may need a "jump-start" in knowing that for which they should be thankful. Here is a partial list. Look at the Bible references to sense the value of blessings we often overlook.

- On behalf of those who minister to you (2 Corinthians 9:11).
- For your food (John 6:11).
- For the mercy of God (Psalms 106:1).
- For the power of the Lord Jesus Christ (Revelation 11:17).
- Because of your deliverance from sin (Romans 7:23-25).
- For wisdom and might (Daniel 2:23).
- For the victory of the Gospel (2 Corinthians 2:14).
- When others are saved (Romans 6:17).
- For other people's faith (2 Thessalonians 1:3).
- For the zeal shown by others (2 Corinthians 8:16).
- When God's presence is near (Psalms 75:1).
- For the willingness, God gives us to offer our resources for His use (1 Chronicles 29:6-14).
- For the supply of our bodily needs (Romans 14:6-7).

There are others, but this list gives you much for which to be appreciative.

Think About It!

1. Try the *Gratitude Journal* mentioned earlier, even if you do not usually write things down. Your *Gratitude Journal* can be as simple as a spiral-bound notebook. The discipline of writing that for which you are thankful raises your awareness. You will begin looking for human kindness and God's blessings for which to be grateful.

2. Lot did not say, "Thank you," to Abram. You be different; be thankful! Thank people who help or bless you in even the smallest way. Your thanks can at least be verbal.

3. A better approach is to express gratitude with a hand-written note. Bishop Paul Mooney's thank you notes are written on any paper at hand. I've received several such messages through the years. One was on a napkin, another on the corner of a page from a legal pad. The paper does not matter. Being thankful does.

4. Write a hand-written "thankful letter" to people who have invested in your life. I've written such encompassing letters to my parents and mentors.

Chapter 16
The Decision Never Made

From Genesis 14:6, until chapter 19, Lot is not mentioned. Twenty years elapsed between Genesis 14 and Genesis 19. ("Life of Abraham Timeline." *We are Israel.* Web. March 9, 2020.) We know nothing about these years of Lot's life, but some things are clear:

- Lot lived in Sodom.
- Lot's children were older. Two of his daughters' married men of Sodom.
- Lot became more prosperous.
- Now in Sodom over two decades, Lot became a leader.
- Sodom's sinfulness increased to the point of gaining God's attention.

In chapter 19, Lot returns to center stage.

> *And there came two angels to Sodom at even; and Lot sat in the gate of Sodom: and Lot seeing them rose up to meet them; and he bowed himself with his face toward the ground; . . . And he pressed upon them greatly; and they turned in unto him, and entered into his house; and he made them a feast, and did bake unleavened bread, and they did eat,* (Genesis 19:1-3).

When Lot saw the two travelers, he greeted them in a way typical to Middle Eastern culture. Lot's invitation for the two to stay in his home was not unusual. Such hospitality was much the case in an ancient setting where there were few inns.

Lot, *"pressed upon them greatly."* When they accepted, Lot was a perfect host. He provided:

- A roof over their head.
- Water with which to wash their feet.
- An extravagant meal.

Did Lot insist the two stay at his home because he knew what would happen if they stayed on the streets? Any overnight guest in Sodom was endangered.

> *But before they lay down, the men of the city, even the men of Sodom, compassed the house round, . . . And they called unto Lot, and said . . . ,, Where are the men which came in to thee this night? bring them out unto us, that we may know them,* (Genesis 19:4-5).

After dinner, a crowd gathered outside Lot's home. This mob ordered Lot to send out his guests, *"that we may know them."* The "men of the city" intended to sexually assault Lot's guests.

Was this the first time this had happened in Sodom? Doubtful! The Sodomites had raped others who traveled through Sodom. On this night, word spread, "Out-of-towners are at Lot's house." The men of Sodom became predators.

Lot had <u>decided</u> to live where brutal sexual attacks were routine.

> Lot had <u>decided</u> to return to Sodom after being rescued from King Chedorlaomer.

> > Lot had <u>decided</u> he wanted to be influential in a city that celebrated perverted sexuality.

Just as Significantly

<center>Lot <u>decided</u> to stay!</center>

Each day was an opportunity to relocate. Perhaps without conscious thought, Lot decided to stay.

Were immorality, homosexuality, and violence now normal to Lot? It happens. In time, it became easier for Lot to stay than leave. No action was needed for Lot's family to remain.

Is this your reality? Is it now more comfortable to continue following a wrong course than to act for change decisively? Casual Christianity is so easy. To worship for two hours each Sunday, while living in a moral pigsty the other 166 hours of a week takes no effort.

Every man needs to take a mental step. Look at your life as though from the outside. What do you see that disgusts or frightens? Satan blinds the eye and numbs the spirit to what surrounds.

Think About It!

1. Reflect upon Lot's willingness to subject his family to a violent, perverted environment to feed his ego of being one of the elders sitting at the city gates. Is your ego a higher priority than your family's safety?
2. Is your status in the community more important than protecting the innocence and purity of your children?
3. To what degree are you going along with what has become the usual, although what surrounds you is not godly?

Chapter 17
Buying Fool's Gold

Fool's gold is well-named. In an earlier time, investors might buy a mineral claim containing what seemed to be gold. Later, they would discover the truth. What they thought was valuable was, in reality, just junk. It was fool's gold.

Men and Fool's Gold

Men choose fool's gold when they highly value the insignificant.

- It is the man who highly values his son's athletic prowess but ignores whether the boy does his homework.
- It is the man who would drive a vehicle and dress his family in a way that makes everyone think him well-to-do; meanwhile, he is drowning in debt.
- It is the man who must win every argument, no matter how insignificant, though his belligerence alienates those who would be his friend.
- It is the man who wants to know more about what is going on than anyone else. He suspects what he does not know. And he tells as fact what he suspects.
- It is the man who imagines himself powerful and well-thought of. In truth, the man is seldom thought of and has little influence.

Lot's Gold

Lot sought significance and found it. It is believed that Lot was designated as a judge. Such men usually sat in the gate of their city. A preacher of another generation called Lot, "the mayor of Sodom." In Sodom, Lot had become somebody!

Lot was a man of influence in a city known for its sin (Genesis 18:20-21). He was prominent where perversion was so universal that the city's name has been used for millennia to refer to homosexuality.

Lot was famous in a town that generations later was named as a place of pride, idleness, and with no concern for the needy, (Ezekiel 16:49-50). But Lot was influential and significant! Or was he?

The Testing of Lot's Gold

How necessary was Lot to the governmental workings of Sodom? Did his opinion matter? Had Lot's years in Sodom made the place better? We don't know but we can imagine.

When Abraham interceded for Sodom and Gomorrah, there were not ten righteous people. Lot, his wife, two married daughters, and two unmarried daughters, totaled six. Perhaps even those were not all righteous. At best, in over twenty years, Lot had not influenced four more people toward right-living.

Men of good influence produce positive change. Lot did not. Lot's influence, importance, and significance looked real. But it was not; Lot was self-deceived. You see this on two occasions.

<u>Lot could not protect his guests.</u> The Sodomites gathered at Lot's home, intending to assault his guests (Genesis 19: 4-5). The two angels being visitors in the house of someone famous, like "Judge Lot" did not restrain the mob. In reality, Lot had little influence.

Second, <u>Lot was not taken seriously</u> by his sons-in-law. When Lot told his sons-in-law to escape because Sodom was about to be destroyed, they ignored him. The young men thought him foolish. *"But his sons-in-law thought he was joking,"* (Genesis 19:14 CEB).

In one day, Lot's self-identity as a powerful man in Sodom crashed. Lot had discovered that his prosperity, position, preferences, and voice meant nothing. Lot had spent decades accumulating fool's gold.

The Judge Became the Jester

In less than 24 hours, Lot went from judge to jester. What influence Lot felt he had was a wisp of air. It was gone. His neighbors did not respond to his leadership, and his sons-in-law thought him a jokester.

Did Lot long to be known as a man of significance? Did he go along to get along? Some men do. They chase what has no meaning for time or eternity. Such men are like Lot; because of the inherent compromises in their approach, they make no impact on those about them.

Gaining Good Gold

Gold has characteristics not present in fool's gold. Prospectors have the equipment to assess what they hold. They do not decide based on the glitter. Men have long since learned, "All that glitters is not gold."

Where can a man be sure to find "good gold"? The Bible, its wisdom, and the decisions to which it guides is gold:

⁷The law of the LORD is perfect,... the testimony of the LORD is sure,... ⁸The statutes of the LORD are right,... the commandment of the LORD is pure,... ⁹...the judgments of the LORD are true and righteous altogether. **¹⁰More to be desired are they than gold, yea, than much fine gold:...,** (Psalm 19:7-10).

What then is your relationship with God's word? If what it contains is better than fine gold, is this not worth pursuing? How is your time of personal devotion? Would you be able to determine a false doctrine if you heard it?

It all comes from the gold of the word of God.

Think About It!

1. Take a slow trip through the Bible. Read and then study one paragraph of the Bible each day. This leisurely trip will take longer than ten years. Make notes, and write down your questions. You will gain far more than you would by reading five chapters daily. Encountering the "good gold" of the Bible brings incremental gains in understanding and application.

2. Show your wife and children the value of knowing God's Word by designating one evening a week as game night. Make Bible learning fun. Play *Bible Trivia*, compete in sword drills, or Bible

word searches on particular chapters. Read a Bible story from a children's book and discuss it. Find a Bible-themed jigsaw puzzle and put it together as a family.

3. During daily devotions, select one or more verses that stand out to you for memorization. Record them in the voice memos of your phone and listen to them several times a day. At the end of one year, you will have memorized at least 365 verses.

4. Have you ever wanted a position or job only to discover that having that job was not what you thought it might be? Lot did. I wonder how Lot felt when his counsel was rejected and his safety threatened? How did your discovery leave you feeling?

Chapter 18
Devalued Children

For children, life is seldom "just a game." A parent's words, deeds, and attitudes have implications beyond a given day.

Lexus Stagg did not intend for it to happen. It was just a game; the three kids loved it. How wonderful it was to see the children laughing so heartily. Just a game.

Except it became more than "just a game." Unfortunately, the game left her 3-year-old son dead. Lexus's three children were playing *chicken* with their mom. The children would dodge out of the way as their mom came toward them.

The game was more than a bit one-sided. Lexus was in her Lincoln Navigator. She repeatedly drove the Lincoln toward her three kids while they ran toward the big SUV. The children would jump aside until the time when Lexus's youngest didn't jump quick enough.

The 26-year-old mother is charged with killing her son, but it was, "just a game." Lexus loved her 3-year-old little boy. Video footage would show her in spasms of grief.

Actions and Outcomes

Actions have outcomes. For Lexus, "chicken" involving a 3-ton Lincoln was a game, but to a little boy, it was life or death. Lexus never intended for her baby to die, but what happened cannot be labeled an accident. The 3-year-old child became collateral damage to a parent, not considering all potential outcomes.

Lack of intent never eliminates responsibility. Lexus is deemed at fault for her son's death. And, Lot bears most of the blame for what happened to his wife and daughters.

The Need to Impress

Men are perpetually competitive. The competition plays out in varied ways; cars, guns, homes, education, money, power, antiques, sports, boats, chess, and a million other ways. As dumb as the mindset is, composer Irving Berlin's catchy phrase, "Anything you can do, I can do better," describes the male way of thinking.

No man wants to look bad in front of other men. And some will make "deals with the devil" to ensure they look better than someone else. Our need to impress shows up in such silly ways:

- You are putting your family in debt to buy a new car. Why? Well, Sam Jones, just down the street, has a new car.
- Did you spend a paycheck on a more powerful rifle, while your car insurance is unpaid. Why? A fellow in the hunting club bought a gun better than mine. I had to keep up.
- Pushing to set a personal high by deadlifting 250 pounds. Your doctor said, "Be careful; your back can't handle too much strain." But you do it anyway. Why? The guy who goes to the gym with you lifted 240 pounds, and you can't let him beat you.
- Playing basketball with teenagers like you were 22 years old, rather than 42. Why? You need to show you've still got it.

The drive to impress, can result in a man making bad choices. Is that what happened to Lot? As the mob demanded Lot's guests be brought out, Lot stepped out to appease the crowd. He said, *"I pray you, brethren, do not so wickedly . . . unto these men do nothing; for therefore came they under the shadow of my roof,"* (Genesis 19:6-8). Under the code of hospitality, these travelers were to experience no harm while under his roof.

Lot's goal was noble. But, it is not easy to deter a violent mob. Furthermore, lust had enflamed this group. The mob would not be deterred and expressed their disdain for Lot.

Imbalanced Decisions

His standing in the community has accomplished nothing, so faced with a gang of men intent on sexual violence, Lot made an inexcusable offer:

> *Behold now, I have two daughters which have not known man; let me, I pray you, bring them out unto you, and do ye to them as is good in your eyes:...* (Genesis 19:8)

Lot "played chicken" with his daughters' well-being. He offered his two virgin daughters for a crowd of lust-filled, violent men to do, *"as is good in your eyes."* As this was all happening, two groups of eyes were on Lot. One group was Lot's neighbors with whom he imagined he had influence. The other eyes were those of the two guests in his home.

Consider this from a "man's man" perspective. Lot was responsible for protecting his guests. Would Lot's manhood, his sense of strength and sufficiency be suspect if he could not protect them? And what about this group standing in front of him? As far as Lot knew, he would be doing business with these people in the future.

Was Lot looking for a way to save face? Perhaps Lot was negotiating to protect his persona. If so, Lot's image, identity, manliness, and saving face had become more important than his daughters.

How far would you go to protect how others see you? Undoubtedly not as far as Lot. Does Lot seem a bit arrogant? Remember how he had decades earlier disrespected both his uncle and neighbors? Lot stole grass from the Canaanites, acting as if the place belonged to him when he was only a guest.

Arrogant men are often dumb about their "man card." Such guys wouldn't give their daughter to rapists, but under pressure from a friend, they'll go fishing rather than make their wedding anniversary special. To be "somebody" with his buds, an arrogant man suddenly decides to go golfing or shooting. His 9-year old son left in tears because Dad was his ride to the baseball game. The one Dad had promised to stay to watch him play.

Lot sold out his family to "save face." Men can make decisions that throw away valuable, unique, and precious "Dad" opportunities just to "win at the *man* game." It's foolish. Only a tiny bit better than the game of "chicken," Lexus played with her three children. Did Lexus win at "chicken!" I suppose, but with such wins, you also lose. Lexus' win destroyed her 3-year-old son.

Men need to get over arrogant egotism. Be a winner in your family responsibilities. Commit to what matters for the long term. How your best friend, neighbor, or co-worker sees you is less important than protecting and providing for your family.

Don't be as Lot, who was willing to trade his children for a bit of community goodwill!

Think About It!

1. Think of an arrogant man, you know. How does he act toward his family? Have you ever seen him sacrifice his family to protect his pride? How did this happen?

2. This chapter mentioned the "man card." Men tease each other about being sure they retain their manhood. That the "little lady" doesn't run their life and to not be a wimp.

   Few Christian men fall prey to that sort of thinking, but many in the world do. You have seen it at work. How do men intimidate other men about such things? Why does arrogance so easily manipulate men?

Chapter 19
Lot – the Toxic Father

In Northeast Louisiana, authorities arrested a man for pimping out his daughters and granddaughters. There was much hue and cry over his control and abuse of adult children and granddaughters in their late teens. People were understandably upset at a "Daddy Pimp" who prostituted his daughters.

Mental health professionals speak of the mental, physical, emotional, and physical scars to a girl manipulated into prostitution. That the exploitation by the "Daddy Pimp" came from the man God intended to be the family provider and protector, would have made those wounds more severe.

The daughters and granddaughters of "Daddy Pimp" will escape the damage of their experiences only through the help of the Lord Jesus Christ.

Remember, what Lot decided to offer as he negotiated to protect his guests.

> *Behold now, I have two daughters which have not known man; let me, I pray you, bring them out unto you, and do ye to them as is good in your eyes* (Genesis 19:8)

In one sentence, Lot showed how much his daughters meant to him. Lot's language is personal, *"Let me . . . bring them out to you."* He seeks no restraint, *". . . do ye to them as is good in your eyes."*

Can you imagine the pinballing, confused thoughts of two teenagers, as they overheard their father tell a gang of rapists that they could do whatever they wished to them? Instead of being a father who was willing to die to protect his family, Lot took down every restraint to actions that would damage his daughters. He actively encouraged their brutal deflowering. How would that betrayal make them feel? Especially as the betrayal came from their father.

Surely they felt:

- Fearful about the unknown.
- Fearful of men who had been neighbors for their entire life.
- Fearful of the tension and violence that filled the air.
- Enraged at their father.
- Violated.
- Devalued.
- Humiliated.
- Insignificant; a tradable commodity.
- Abandoned to pain and savagery.
- Unworthy of protection.
- Less important than two unknown guests.
- Undeserving of love.

Lot was not "Pimp Daddy" offering his daughters to anonymous men for paid sex. He wanted to give them to men bent on violent rape. To what degree had the perversions common to Sodom affected Lot's mind? Would Lot have made a similar offer if Abraham had been his primary influencer for the past decades? It seems unlikely.

Words Wound - Forever

You have heard the adage, "Sticks and stones may break my bones, but words will never hurt me." That proverb is a lie. Words hurt; Lot's words wounded his daughters. Their minds and spirits had gaping wounds that affected their trust of men. It diminished their respect for themselves.

Fathers wound with words. Just because you didn't mean what you said doesn't mean it does not hurt. Nor does it mean the hurt does not last. Hard words leave "bruises that are all on the inside." Children require emotional nurturing. With Lot's daughters getting the exact opposite; how could they have developed any sense of self-worth.

Children Believe What You Say

Some fathers attack their children directly. In private and often in public, they viciously degrade their kids by using words like stupid, worthless, or ugly. Others, equally assault their child with a deadly barrage of teasing sarcasm, insulting nicknames, and putdowns. Such dads then excuse the words by saying, "It was just a joke."

Listen: Children cannot distinguish when you are joking. The brain of a child is still developing. Logic and reasoning have not been established in your nine-year-old, nor even in your twelve-year-old. Your child takes your sarcasm and malicious jokes at face value.

Children are sponges, absorbing the words you say, as well as your non-verbal messages. They listen, watch, and imitate their parents. Lot's words makes his daughters available to rapists were hurtful.

Fortunately, Lot's daughters did not experience rape. But it was not for lack of Lot making the two girls available. Sodom's perverted men rejected Lot's virgin daughters. They only desired Lot's guests.

But Lot's words, like those of every parent, were living things. Parents should bless their children as Abraham, Isaac, and Jacob blessed their sons. Do parents not curse their children when they communicate the child's insignificance?

How could a woman have a good self-image when her father had so treated her? Wouldn't Lot's daughters think, "If our father feels we are of no higher value than to potentially subject us to pain, savagery, humiliation, emotional, verbal, and mental abuse, how can any other man think we have significance?"

The humiliating words Lot loosed that night could never be unsaid. They would soon echo in a mountain cave above Zoar, and Lot's devaluing words would have implications for a millennium to come.

On Lot's last evening in Sodom, he stripped his daughters of their self-esteem.

STOP destroying with your words!

- STOP berating your wife and kids. Listen to what you are saying. Do you curse or give a blessing?
- STOP critiquing your kids before others. Whether family members, friends, or casual acquaintances. Don't publicly humiliate your kids to make yourself look better.
- STOP tearing down every effort your son or daughter makes at something new. They may enter a different field of life than you. Support them in attempting new things.
- STOP belittling your son for missing the deer, even if his attempt knocked the top from a tree. Making your children the butt of a joke tears them down.
- STOP comparing your children with others at school and church. The phrase, "Why aren't you more like . . ." is to be eradicated from your vocabulary.
- STOP bullying your family to "show them you are the boss." A man's God-given authority is first in the spiritual realm. Get in a prayer room and gain victory over the world, the flesh, and the devil. Then authority at home will seem to happen automatically.

Toxic Fathers

That which is toxic taints what it touches. Toxic land will not grow healthy vegetables. No subdivisions are built on toxic acreage.

Toxic parents consistently express negative patterns of harmful behavior. Can you think of one decision Lot got right? Every decision was to benefit himself. For decades Lot had not considered others. The Canaanites experienced his dishonesty; Abram encountered Lot's disrespect and lack of gratitude, and in Sodom, Lot's ambitions always outweighed his responsibility to his family. Lot was a toxic father.

Of the traits common among toxic parents, Lot displayed several:

- Inadequacy – Lot was so focused on his problem that he hoped his daughters could be used to take care of his problem. A child having to cover for or lie about Dad's lacking is toxic inadequacy. Lot did not care how much using them as sex-slaves would wound his daughters – all to fix his problem.
- Control – Lot knew he could command his daughters, and they would obey. Toxic fathers commonly use manipulation and emotional blackmail to be the puppet-master in their child's life.
- Verbal Abuse – Lot's offering of his girls to the mob served to diminish their self-worth. Wounding words tear down children.
- Devaluation – Devaluing another person makes them feel insignificant. The child is of no consequence, and their pain or disappointment never matters. Your words and actions can both devalue.
- Disrespect – Public discipline of an older child is toxic. The youngster never forgets the humiliation. Are there not better ways to correct a child's behavior?
- Destructive – Some men do not want their children to rise above their station in life. So the child receives no support, and their future is sabotaged; dreams are not encouraged, instead they are mocked. A favored phrase is, "What makes you think you could . . . ?" Ideas and dreams are shattered.
- Sexual Abuse – Lot's flagrantly sexual treatment of his daughters was abuse. He objectified his daughters as pawns on a chessboard, a commodity to use.

Sexual Abuse

Sexual violation of a child is a genuinely evil act. (Forward, Susan with Buck, Craig. *Toxic Parents - Overcoming Their Hurtful Legacy and Reclaiming Your Life.* pp. 138.) By that measure, Lot was a genuinely evil man. He intended to facilitate the sexual violation of his daughters. Men who sexually abuse family members impact that person for a lifetime.

In the book of Judges, a man's concubine, taken in a situation not dissimilar to the one in Sodom, died as a result of being repeatedly and violently raped (Judges 19:25-28). Her treatment was vile and vicious. Rape and sexual assault are about violence, power, and control rather than the rapist's sexual satisfaction. It is the rapist showing, "This is what I can do to you, and get away with it."

Sexual abuse of a child violates innocence solely for the abuser's gratification. Lot's willingness to offer his girls put their lives at risk and communicated the following evil feelings toward them:

1. Look what I'm able to do with you if I so choose.
2. Here is the value I place on you.
3. How others perceive me - these guests - is more important than your health, well-being, and life.
4. Peace outside the home is more important than being trusted by my children.

Such violation is not necessarily physical. A parent's sexually charged comments or innuendo are invasive. Telling your daughter how "hot" she looks carries a sexual connotation, and she knows it. When instead, you tell your daughter she is "beautiful" and that you are thankful she is your daughter you have provided healthy affirmation.

Unsafe Fathers

Where there is no sense of safety, there is also no sense of security. Although you should want your children to respect and obey you, they should not live with a cowering fear of you. If you are an unsafe father, you multiply your children's fears.

- Fear of not being loved.
- Fear of failure.
- Fear of being rejected by other people.
- Fear of marriage.

- Fear of disapproval.
- Fear of the future.
- Fear of sexual assault and violence.
- Fear of never getting married.
- Fear of success.
- Fear of humiliation.
- Fear of men.

Fear is the opposite of faith. Raising children to fear is horrid because it prevents them from establishing deep relationships. Anxiety becomes a trap from which they feel unable to escape. Dad, if you don't protect and project your child toward a secure and positive future, who will?

Did Lot's control tactics crush the spirit of his two younger daughters? At the time, they had no control over whether or not they would be offered to the evil men of Sodom. However, when they gained control on the mountain above Zoar, they quickly moved into inappropriate sexual behavior.

It is incredible how fears go back to childhood. The daughter of an alcoholic wrote him, "I often felt your love for alcohol kept you from loving me. That is where my fear of never being loved came from."

Might one of Lot's daughters have written to him, "I often felt your love for being well thought of and respected in Sodom kept you from loving me?"

Safe Men

Daughters need a safe man in their life. Their dad is the right man to be the first of their safe men. Safe people listen when you talk. You know they will protect you even at a cost to themselves. Safe men don't bring information into their daughter's life that would corrupt her morals before she understands what morals are. R-rated movies, sexual language, suggestive books, and magazines don't come to a safe dad's address.

No father gets it right all the time. Men are not always emotionally available. It's normal for parents to yell at their children at times. In fear of our children's well-being or due to our own selfishness, fathers may on occasion be too controlling.

There were times when I failed as a father. Those times sometimes resurface in my memory. It would be great to be able to relive those times, but such is not the nature of life. I've asked my sons to forgive me for specific bad choices. Lane and Chris did not even remember the events that were bothering me. But since it bothered me, they forgave me.

If you have made similar wrong decisions, would it not be right to address those with your children? Your confessions will help them realize that you are aware of your imperfections as a father.

The Outcome of Toxic Parenting

Fathers are responsible to provide for and protect their families. It seems unrealistic to imagine Lot having reliably protected his daughters, then offering them to be treated with such violence.

How did Lot decline? We can't know, but it is clear that Lot's thinking was flawed. In Sodom, sexual sin was ordinary; same-sex relationships were common, and from what we have read in Genesis, sexual violence was an accepted practice.

Lot now thought like the citizens of Sodom. Sexual messages had affected him to the point where no barriers remained. Allowing influences like those in Sodom's to be your guide will do that to a man. If twenty years earlier, you had said to Lot, "Sir, in a few years you will offer your daughters to a mob of men for their sexual pleasure," those would have been fighting words.

Slow incremental steps had brought Lot to this place. Where are your actions leading you?

Think About It!

1. If you are comfortable with it and dare, have a woman read the story of Lot being will to offer his daughters. Ask their response. How did it make them feel toward Lot? If they had been one of Lot's daughters how would it have made them feel?

2. Review the list of things to "stop" doing. How guilty are you of some of these? Do you need to ask someone to help you overcome what may well be a habit?

3. Unfortunately, what we experienced as children we often replicate as parents. When you look at the toxic behavior in this chapter, are there any you regularly experienced? If so, what have you done not to behave this way toward your children?

Chapter 20
Decisions Under Duress

Stress reveals us. When Lot's neighbors demanded his guests to abuse and violate, he protested and offered his two virgin daughters as objects of their lust. The mob did not accept Lot's offer, and the angels rescued him from physical harm.

Under duress, we see two of Lot's default settings. What Lot did not do, and something he instead did pull back the curtain on who Lot now was.

When the pressure is on, a man shows who he is. One man may become sullen and resentful; another man immediately begins to look for solutions; another fellow may do a "runner" to avoid dealing with the state of affairs. Who do you become when things go wrong? What is your instinctive reaction?

Lot Did Not Pray

Decades earlier, Lot had seen God deliver Abram and Sarai from bad situations. The circumstances were usually Abram's fault. Abram had faith, but when he was afraid, he was not always honest. Yet God had rescued him.

Even with years having passed, it seems Lot would have recalled God's help for his imperfect uncle. In every aspect of his life, whether making a decision about his family's future or when facing a matter of personal danger, Lot's default seemed to be, "Don't involve God."

As his longtime neighbors are attacking Lot, he does not appeal for God's help. In our terminology, "The name Jesus was no longer the first thing to Lot's lips." Had Lot forgotten about God's ability to rescue? Did God's power even come to mind?

Lot's default was now, "Life without God." Perhaps not even conscious of the decision, Lot chose not to pray.

Men Who Forget the Altar

Is it not sad when men who twenty years back would first look to Jesus now seek their help from a therapist, banker, attorney, friend, or a myriad of other options? Such men often never think of praying. Oh, they may put "praying hands" beneath a need mentioned on social media. But, if they were asked "when" did you pray about that need, they would have no answer. It is an unfortunate man who forgets the altar.

Did Lot feel so far removed from God that he did not have the privilege of prayer? If so, Lot underestimated Abram's God. The Almighty knew where Lot was. He had not forgotten Lot.

The All-Men's Mercy Club

If you have drifted far from your past relationship with Jesus, it is time to remember Him. Whether you are in crisis or not, it is the right time to call on the Lord Jesus Christ. Perhaps you feel unworthy. Who doesn't?

- His mercy is new each morning (Lamentations 3:22-23)
- His mercy endureth forever (Psalms 106:1)
- *"Where sin abounded grace did much more abound,"* (Romans 5:20).
- Jesus is still faithful and just to forgive your sins and to cleanse you from all unrighteousness (1 John 1:9).

Welcome to the "All-Men's Mercy Club." Jesus is the President of the club, and He turns none away. You will fit right in.

Make your chair, park bench, or roadside an altar. Humbly ask God for forgiveness, mercy, and divine intervention. Jesus has not forgotten you.

In the pressure of the moment, Lot forgot to pray! Don't be that man. God cannot answer any prayer; you do not pray.

Patterns We Follow

Lot's second default was to negotiate in the common currency of Sodom – sexual favors. This currency was familiar to Lot. Some Rabbis say Lot chose to move to Sodom because he wanted to participate in its immorality.

Lot's decisions consistently show a pattern of self-interest. To misuse his daughters to protect two new friends was the ultimate indication of a trend of ongoing selfishness.

Lot did not pray; instead, he tried to bargain with the predators of Sodom. And what Lot offered the Sodomites was not his to give. He was stealing his daughters' rights to marry and give themselves to a man of their choice. It was not the first time for Lot to try to use what was not his.

Patterns! Earlier, Lot had stolen pasture from the Canaanites to fatten his livestock. Decades had passed, but nothing had changed. Lot was like a man using a stolen credit card to pay his bills.

Our Decisions Create a Path

Repeated behavior becomes a beaten path. Given enough time and repetition, your decisions wear a groove in the concrete of your life. Often, our children then travel the same routes.

Lot's daughters assumed a worldview like that of their father. We will see them respond to an imagined "crisis," an immoral solution.

Lot, and later, his daughters believed the end justified the means even if it involved behavior acceptable in no place except Sodom.

Think About It!

1. What is your first response if you are laid off from a job or get a bad report from your doctor?

2. What solutions have you seen men try while they were under high stress? Which worked best? Why?

3. Is there a particular person you appeal to when a problem arises? What has caused you to look to that person?

4. What is your default solution for trying to take care of a problem? Some things men commonly use: money, the power of intimidation, charm, who they know. What others come to mind?

Chapter 21
Consequences of Delay

The death of a friend angered me. I wasn't angry with God. I was mad at my friend, who had diabetes and other health issues. He ate wrong, and exercise was non-existent.

Due to diabetes, my friend had a sore on his leg that developed into a running wound. He was stubborn as a rock. Friends and family encouraged, cajoled, and demanded he visit a doctor. Did I mention he was stubborn as a rock? His response was, "Let's see how it goes. If it is not better soon, I'll go to a doctor." The man delayed getting help. He delayed some more. Then, yet again.

Finally, my friend developed a high fever and could no longer resist the demands to visit an Emergency Room. The diagnosis was quick. Bacteria from the running wound had entered his bloodstream. He was septic. In days, my friend was dead. He needn't have died so soon.

My friend did not die from diabetes or a wound that went septic. He died because of deciding to delay a trip to the doctor. His delay was deadly.

Delay is a decision!

When his neighbors wanted to harm him, Lot's guests pulled him inside his home, and the men outside were blinded. It was then that the angels spoke of Sodom's impending destruction. Lot wanted his family saved and went to warn his married daughters and their husbands (Genesis 19:1-14). Lot's sons-in-law believed he mocked.

The following day, the angels encouraged Lot to leave Sodom quickly:

...then the angels hastened Lot, saying, Arise, take thy wife, and thy two daughters, which are here; lest thou be consumed..., **(Genesis 19:15).**

Lot did not hasten. Genesis 19:16: *And while he (Lot) lingered ....* Lot, like my diabetic friend was delaying. Delay is a decision.

Lot's Uncertainty

Doesn't it seem that Lot was unsure of what to do? His hesitation is surprising, considering:

- His guests having saved him from men intent on harming him (Genesis 19:10)
- The miraculous blinding of the Sodomites (Genesis 19:11)
- A pointed warning that the destruction of Sodom was imminent (Genesis 19:13)
- The angels' warning to, "Hurry up . . . lest thou be consumed" (Genesis 19:15)

All evidence suggested quick action. Yet, Lot lingered.

The first five books of the Bible, called the *Torah* by Jews, do not have a word for *uncertainty*. Instead, to describe *uncertainty*, ancient Hebrew used markings not unlike what would be called a "Flat Sign (♭)" in music.

Various marks of this type are in Hebrew literature. The symbols are not letters of the Hebrew alphabet. Instead, these characters gave emphasis and a subtle explanation about the text.

¹²And the men said unto Lot, Hast thou here any besides? . . . bring them out of this place: ¹³For we will destroy this place, . . . ¹⁴And Lot went out, and spake unto his sons in law, . . . But he seemed as one that mocked. . . ¹⁵And when the morning arose, then the angels hastened Lot, ... ¹⁶And while he lingered, the men laid hold upon his hand, . . . (Genesis 19:12-16).

Above the word translated, "lingered" in verse 16 is a symbol known as a *shalshelet*. This mark expressed indecision. The symbol above a word provided the tone of voice a reader was to use. Pictured to the left is a *shalshelet*. It looks a bit like a zigzag. A word with a *shalshelet* above it was read using a wavering voice that expressed indecision.

- Lot knew he needed to leave Sodom, but he lingered.

- Lot wanted to be safe, but his life was in Sodom.
- Lot's wealth was in Sodom, and his older daughters were in Sodom.

Lot could scarcely move him from the city. Few things in life are inevitable. But those few certain things should compel us to quick action.

- Death and judgment are sure things (Hebrews 9:27).
- The second coming of the Lord Jesus Christ is inevitable (Revelation 22:7, 12).
- The catching away of the church will take place (1 Thessalonians 4:15-17).
- There will be tribulation on the earth (Matthew 24:21-22).
- The antichrist will rule the world (2 Thessalonian 2:1-4; Revelation 13:5-8)

What have you done to respond to these inevitable realities? Many men do as Lot in Sodom. They linger, knowing they need to obey God, but not able to yield to God's direction.

Linger long enough as did my diabetic friend, and you are beyond help. The sure thing becomes a current thing. The opportunity to escape is gone. Stop lingering!

An Uncertain Identity

Men unsure of their identity have a *shalshalet* over their life. Such men remain on the edge of their church, even as revival happens. The quick-step march of Endtime events does not move them to action.

Lot was such a man. Decades earlier, Lot had eagerly pursued what faith had to offer. By chapter 19, Lot had fully embraced life in Sodom. Lot was now a man of the city gates.

Lot knew he had to leave Sodom, just as you realize the necessity of obeying the Lord. The problem, even with tragedy ahead, was that

Lot did not want to leave Sodom. Such men struggle with their identity. Are you a man of this world, hesitant to let go of what you have always valued? Or are you a man of God, ready to respond and release?

Resolved or Unresolved

Abram and Lot contrast. When God directed, Abram acted. Abram was a lifelong pilgrim. Lot pursued "permanence" while Abram was secure that God had spoken. He did not need a permanent address; Abram was comfortable with trusting God.

Lot's roots in Sodom were so deep that Lot self-identified as a judge of the city. What is your self-identity? *"For as he thinketh in his heart, so is he,"* (Proverbs 23:7). Sodom was the city where Lot foresaw living out his days.

Men so rooted, particularly those who once lived by faith, find it hard to obey the Lord, even in the face of death and judgment. Are you rooted in the values of our world? Within hours of Lot having seen the miraculous – still, he lingered!

Lot eventually departed, coerced by the angels. But, even as the small group left Sodom, Lot was still communicating to his wife and daughters how much he valued Sodom. Is there any wonder that his wife looked back?

The Motives to Linger

Lot's entanglements are the sort that causes men to have a *shalshelet* – the symbol of wavering uncertainty – over their life. Knowing better, men become paralyzed by mixed desires.

What motives cause men to linger?

Wealth

   Success

      Identity

         Children who know nothing of God

>> Position

> Roots

Comfort

Lot hard work, two married daughters, position, wealth, and charming home screamed stay. Two strangers, who had performed a notable miracle and were now warning Lot of impending judgment, were whispering, "You have to go."

For a man to linger in the face of a sure thing is folly, it is time to obey God. There will never be a more convenient season. Life only gets more complicated. Time never repairs a man's estrangement from God. Instead, time always moves men further away.

Think About It!

1. Do you remember an opportunity you missed because you waited? What was the outcome? How long before you realized what you had lost.

2. What are the decisions required for you to move closer to the middle of what Jesus is doing?

3. If, like Lot, you are of a mixed mind, causing you to delay your action for God for ten years, what implications is it likely to have for your children?

Beyond Sodom

Chapter 22
Nurturing, Empowering and Protecting

In an ancient vineyard, a husbandman worked to gain health and productivity for the plants. In the marriage relationship, God used the word *husband* by intent. As is the case for every married man, Lot was to "husband" his wife's well-being and health – mentally, emotionally, physically, and spiritually. *Husband* is not only a noun, but it is also a verb calling for action.

Remember the Husband

Remember Lot's wife, invites us to imagine the nurturing Lot provided. What kind of husband do you suppose Lot was? Did being married to Lot make his wife a better person? Abram and Sarai were a team. Does the same seem to be the case for Lot and his wife?

Disobedience caused the death of Lot's wife. She looked back at Sodom and Gomorrah. Her motives are not known; her mindset unclear.

- The couple had two daughters in Sodom. Were they weeping as they waved goodbye? Would it not have been trying for any mom to resist one last look at her children?
- The family wealth was in Sodom. Did Lot's wife think about the financial loss her family was suffering?
- Sodom was part of her identity. She had been there for at least two decades. A wicked environment can be a comfort zone that becomes home.

We can't explain, but Jesus told us to remember.

Responsible Fatherhood

Not only is a married man to husband his wife, but he is also to be a father. A father provides, protects, and prepares his children. God blessed Lot's marriage with four daughters. As a dad, Lot was to provide, protect from harm, and ready his kids for future decisions.

Provide

Lot was wealthy. The children of a wealthy man are usually privileged to enjoy the better things of life. Whatever Lot's children needed was available. They would have experienced the best.

When Sodom was destroyed, Lot's wealth was gone. His family departed with little more than the clothes on their back. Soon Lot and his daughters were residing in a cave.

How did Lot do as a provider? To "provide" means more than clothes and shoes. Did Lot give his children anything regarding the things of God? When you look at Lot's children, what priorities and patterns do they seem to have learned from Lot?

Did Lot's provision position them for the future?

Protect

Lot was no kind of protector. Instead of being a defensive wall around his two girls, Lot negotiated to allow their harm – physically, psychologically, mentally, and emotionally.

What can a man do to protect his children? Some things are obvious. No father would knowingly put his child in the care of a pedophile. You would not suggest they play in a busy street. You'll rise to your child's defense if you discover they are being bullied. But, there is so much more from which to protect them.

How is that a man may fail to protect his family from the destroyer?

1. Are you unaware of who the destroyer(s) are?
2. Have you created intentional barricades to protect your children? There are no "accidental" barriers. If you do not intentionally build a fortress of protection, none will exist.
3. If the choice is my close friends or my children, do I sacrifice my children in any way? The men gathered at Lot's had been his friends.

To what degree have you left your children unprotected?

Prepare

How well have we prepared our children for life? Such preparation is not in evidence when a child is 8, 13, or 16. The evidence is more apparent when your offspring is 23, 25, or 32.

By the early 20s, a mature young adult is no longer warring with their emotions and no longer imagines their parents to be "out of touch." There is evidence of a person's ability to control their feelings and desires. We begin to see their priorities. At this point, the preparation provided by a parent comes into full view.

Little of this sort of preparation happens in a classroom. A child's readiness for these things comes from the example of their parents. Albert Schweizer said there are three ways to teach, "By example, by example, by example." What pattern are you providing?

Lot's example prepared his daughters to make similar bad decisions. What Lot valued, or perhaps conceded to, became meaningful to his girls.

Lot's daughters did not make the right decisions. Lot had not prepared his daughters to make the right decisions. As a father, are you providing an example that will prepare your children to make the right decisions?

Think About It!

1. How well do you provide for your family? Are you diligent at staying employed, or is your wife the consistent source of income? If you have not been the provider repent. Do the right thing. Get a job and stay with it. There will always be things about work that you don't like. Go ahead, accept that this will be the case. Get busy, providing for your family. Can a male even be called a man if he does not support his family?

2. Do you provide them an education about the things of the Lord Jesus Christ? How often do they see you pray? Worship? Read the Bible? Do a work of evangelism?

3. Children sense when they are at risk. Are your kids protected? Do they know it? Have you told them to come to you if someone, even a family member, attempts to involve them in sexual play? Have you assured them you will listen and that no harm will come to them if they share what someone told them had to be "a secret?" A child only feels protected if they sense you will listen to them, believe their story, and act to protect them.

4. Wisdom and folly will both transfer from one generation to the next. Don't assume your children can reason out why you decided as you did. Use teachable moments to give insight about why you choose as you do.

5. Do you tell stories? Not about your grand successes. Best preparation often comes from learning about a parent's wrong decision. The father can then tell them what he should have done differently.

6. Never glorify your foolish misdeeds or sin. When you joke about how much you drank, stole, used drugs, etc. you set your child up to duplicate your lousy behavior. While you may have recovered from a few nights on the town, getting blind drunk, your child could become an alcoholic!

Chapter 23
Deferred Outcomes

There may be deferred outcomes, but there will be an outcome!

Dale and Emmy

Dale and Emmy were the king and queen of the high school class. Dale was the star football player, Emmy was a cheerleader and graduated as the school valedictorian. Their graduating class selected the two as *Most Likely to Succeed*. In retrospect, it seems foregone. Dale and Emmy dated, became sweethearts, and at seventeen were engaged to marry.

Emmy had the grades to pursue a college degree. Dale trained to be a welder. Good-paying jobs were readily available. Unfortunately, Dale was committed to fishing, hunting, and lounging around the house considerably more than work. Emmy had no opportunity for college because Dale decided to be a "red-neck playboy." Emmy became the family breadwinner. Her job as a nurse's aide paid little. Sons were born.

At times, Dale would enthusiastically get a welding job, usually to save money for a big-screen television or a new aluminum boat. Dale's family finances never improved. They never owned anything of significance, and their home was one decrepit place after another. Dale became obese, a man with diabetes and chronic gout. His health got so bad he was not employable.

The couple voted, "Most Likely to Succeed," failed in almost everything. Dale's decision to be a lazy ne'er-do-well left his family in poverty. Emmy became embittered, her brilliant mind, unchallenged and wasted. The potential within her to be a doctor, nurse, or electrical engineer moldered on the shelf. Emmy mentally survived by reading every library book she could get her hands on.

Dale, as a role model, resulted in his sons doing much the same thing. Joey, the older son, added addiction to the toxic equation. He married a lady who had experienced violent abuse. Her primary method of communication was a screaming fit, followed by throwing hard objects. Joey responded in kind. Dale's son is a lazy, unproductive addict living in a mutually abusive marriage. The couple and their two sickly children live on funds provided by the country's taxpayers.

Shane, the younger son, left the area. It was not as though he shot for the stars. He joined the circus and traveled as a roustabout. Shane experimented with alcohol, drugs, and various forms of bizarre sexual behavior. At least, Shane had a job.

Dale and Emmy were church members. She was perpetually haggard from hard work, frustration, and disappointment. Dale consistently attended church. That is always the right decision! But, long before he attended church for the first time, Dale had decided to be a lazy ne'er do well. He never repented of laziness. As my dad would say, "Dale was just *sorry*."

Dale's decision to be irresponsible and not carry the load for his wife and sons was long-tailed. As the late Evangelist Doyle Spears often preached, "There is a Payday Someday!" Today, Dale's decisions affect three generations. The influence of Dale's decisions may extend much farther.

Dale's wife has much in common with Lot's wife. Lot's wife becoming a pillar of salt at least in part, came as a result of her husband's earlier decisions. You can trace the bitter weariness of Dale's wife and the unfortunate outcome for their sons back to Dale's choices.

Lot's Wife

Jesus focused his listener's attention when He said, "Remember Lot's wife." She deserves remembering. In Jewish synagogues, the story of the woman's disobedience and demise is often read.

We know of one decision made by Lot's wife. Her one recorded decision left her a pillar of salt.

Meanwhile, Lot's life was a parade of bad decisions. Lot's choices helped shape his wife. How could it not be so? Lot's bad judgments set his wife up for failure. Think about the consequences of Lot's actions.

- What if Lot's wife had never lived in Sodom? It was Lot who decided to become a citizen of Sodom.
- What if Lot had not been willing to bring up his four daughters in a city known for pride, selfishness, sexual perversion, and violence? But Lot was ready to surround his children with the perverse.
- What if Lot had never sought to increase his wealth in the plains along the Jordan River? But Lot did pursue wealth!
- What if Lot had not been ambitious to gain influence in Sodom? But Lot liked being one of the judges in the city gate.
- What it . . . ?

How did Lot's wife end as she did? Lot's self-absorbed decisions positioned his wife and all four children for disaster.

Lot's decisions affected a millennium. Dale's decisions may do the same; your choices have the same possibility. Choose well, sir, please choose well.

Think About It!

1. When you consider the potential that Emmy had to be involved in something meaningful like scientific research, or as a missionary, how do you suppose she felt toward Dale's laziness?
2. In what ways can a husband nurture his wife? Be specific. Think of ways you can encourage your wife to fulfill her potential and enjoy using the talents and gifts God gave her.

Chapter 24
Sodom's Survivors

The Bible does not leave out the ugly, and there is a lot of ugly in Genesis 19. At Lot's request, God did not destroy the town of Zoar (Genesis 19:20-24) not far from Sodom.

Imagine the scene. Dawn had scarcely broken when fire and brimstone fell on Sodom and Gomorrah. A fireball reached hundreds of yards upward. The people of Zoar were horrified. Some began running toward Sodom, hoping to rescue survivors. Others afraid that more fire may come and reach to Zoar, ran in the opposite direction, putting distance between themselves and Sodom.

The stench of sulfur permeated the air. As the fires burned, cinders and ash floated down. There was the acrid smell of burning flesh.

When the shock of the surreal passed, people started thinking in terms of human loss. Most had family or friends who lived in Gomorrah or Sodom. Then questions, wrought with emotion began:

- I wonder if Grandma made it out?
- Do you suppose Dad had already got to Sodom with the oats he was taking to market?
- Do you think anybody survived?

Those who started toward Sodom to rescue survivors returned home pressed back by the intense heat. They were sadly shaking their heads, saying, "Nobody could have got out of that alive!" But someone had.

Unexpected Survivors

Lot and his two daughters arrived in Zoar. They were filthy. Ash and filth were in the girl's hair. Layers of soot covered them.

Upon seeing the three survivors, some ran to meet them. Each person was hoping that one of the three was their father, mother, or child. It was not the case. Disappointed, most of those who had run out to meet them sank deeper into despair. A few more hearty souls stepped up to help Lot and his daughters.

The hours passed. Lot and his kids were cleaned up, given food and water, their cuts and bruises tended. The people of Zoar had learned their names, where they had lived, and what sort of work Lot had done. Because Lot had been a "man of the gate," he was known to some in Zoar.

How often was Lot asked, "What happened?" Do you suppose Lot told them that the fire and brimstone was the judgment of God and that a warning to leave had come to him? I don't imagine he did.

With each passing hour, hope for more survivors decreased. Despair and gloom settled on Zoar. The stench became acrider, the sense of loss more pronounced. Grief-stricken wails began to sound as people realized they'd never see their loved ones again.

How long was it before someone gave further thought to the three survivors? In a catastrophe, people seek someone to blame. Would Lot not being a native of the plains, though he had been there for decades, make him suspect. People are also superstitious. The murmurs increased, "Three people survived, none of the three are actually from Sodom. Doesn't that seem odd to you?"

Further Flight

Soon, Lot became "afraid to stay in Zoar," and moved on. Decades earlier, by moving into Sodom, Lot had forsaken life as a vagabond. But after leaving Zoar, Lot's next home was a cave. His wealth and prestige were gone. All pretense of success had vanished.

Lot had made decisions aiming for what he considered being a success. And for decades, it seemed to have worked. But now, Lot's achievements are gone.

Success is When Jesus Says, "Well Done!"

An adage says, "Don't count your chickens before they hatch." Isn't that what Lot did? While in Sodom, Lot felt comfortable and secure regarding the future. All was well; Lot's decisions had got him what he wanted. But, when his life came apart, Lot's accumulation of fool's gold bought him nothing.

Men who measure their life by assets, collections, famous friends, position, prestige, and success, tend to mark their life as a "win" before the game is over. In one day, a corporate bankruptcy connected with fraud can eliminate your retirement account; a doctor's report can make you willing to trade all you own for five years of a healthy life. Your teenage daughter, whose golf game and singing skills you crowed about to your friends, can be an empty-eyed meth addict when she is 25.

Like Lot, what we had presumed to be settled was not settled at all. And tragedy burns bitterness into the human spirit.

Some like Lot, never include God, God's will, righteousness, or integrity in their decisions. And just as was the case for Lot, they will suffer loss.

Again, Abram is the perfect contrast. By the time Lot moved to a cave, God had renamed Abram, giving him the name Abraham. The wanderer from Ur would become the father of nations. He had plodded through life, being obedient to God.

> Abraham, a man of faith, established a people and race that even now endure. Through Abraham's legacy, blessings came to all nations of the earth.

> Lot, a selfish man, was consumed by the visible world, but in the end, he retained none of its valuables. Lot's only legacy is a compilation of bad decisions.

Which had you rather be? Abram, with the life of a pilgrim but leaving behind an admirable report. Or Lot, consistently deciding on what would give him success yet dying a failure.

Instead, the question should be; which of the two men are you like right now? If you don't like the answer, what do you need to change?

Think about It!

1. As a resident of Sodom, Lot had much prestige. After Sodom was destroyed, Lot had nothing to show for his life's work. What emotions, do you suppose, ran through Lot on the day he moved into a cave?
2. Did Lot have anything to fear from the residents of Zoar? Fear can be irrational. Why might Sodom's three survivors have been looked at suspiciously?
3. Consider Lot's surviving daughters. How did they feel about Lot? Do you suppose they realized that their father had positioned them for disaster? Did they fault him? To what degree do you blame your parents for any challenges in your life?
4. If you continue to make decisions as you have for the past ten years, will your children have reason to feel you consistently made bad choices?

Chapter 25
The Decision of the Second Night

When Lot and his daughters left Zoar, he was a pauper living in fear of the people in the nearest town. Due to disobedience, the wife with whom he had raised four daughters had been turned into a pillar of salt. Lot's two oldest daughters were dead, their bodies hidden in brimstone.

The emotional toll on Lot would have been massive. Lot's daughters were also suffering. In a crisis, a daughter needs her mom. But she wasn't there. Less critical, but gone were the jewels and beautiful clothes. Any finery they had possessed was now ash. In a matter of hours, life had changed.

In Sodom, Lot had household help. On the mountain, they were alone. In a few hours, the life of Lot's daughters had gone from grand to grimy, grubby manual labor.

A Man Alone

Lot had enjoyed the camaraderie of other men. Lot liked being in the gate of the city, laughing, talking, hearing the latest gossip, or tall-tale. Also, as a "man of the gate," Lot had been participating in what seemed to be meaningful decisions.

Most men like companionship with other men. It may be a hunting club, a foursome on a golf course, lunch with a group of peers, an early morning prayer meeting followed by breakfast, being on a "basketball team for geezer's only," bike-riding together, or riding your Harleys for a day.

These connections are essential. Isolated men are dangerous; to themselves and others. Any man who has been used to interacting with other men, but now alone suffers an acute loss.

Lot was such a man.

- When men laugh together, teasing, cajoling, and joking, it is refreshing. Lot had no man with whom to laugh.

- When men can talk together, ideas are shared, and wrong thinking is corrected. Lot had no man with whom to talk.
- When men can seek the counsel of another man, options are considered, and the pros and cons of a course of action are contemplated. Lot had no man with whom to counsel.
- When men are together, one man may sense another man's despair and speak an encouraging word. Lot had no man to sense his desperation.
- When men congregate, there is a sharing of hopes and possibilities. The man who sees no way up or out will often have another man do something that raises him. Lot had no man to lift him.

Isolation by Choice

Given the circumstances, Lot's separation from other men seems unavoidable. Regardless, Lot would have missed his friends.

Lot had no choice. There are times when men choose to isolate themselves. It raises concern when a man decides to no longer company with other Christian men. Instead, he separates, closing in on himself. He does not answer the phone or reply when sent a text. He returns no calls.

An isolated Christian is a vulnerable Christian, and Satan knows it. Many reasons cause a man to choose isolation. Personal sin, embarrassment at a business failure, disappointment over a church decision, being offended by the pastor or some other church member, and a myriad of other reasons have caused men to decide to isolate themselves from their brothers.

Regardless of the reason, isolation by choice is always a "bad decision." Jesus taught, "offense will come." I've been offended, and I've been the offender. But I don't want to be alone. No man needs to be alone, and we need each other.

Unlike Lot, you have a choice, don't isolate yourself from other men.

Irrational Decisions

Lot and his daughters were alone on the mountain.

> [30] *And Lot went up out of Zoar, . . . and he dwelt in a cave, he and his two daughters.* [31] *And the firstborn said unto the younger, Our father is old, and there is not a man in the earth to come in unto us after the manner of all the earth:* [32] *Come, let us make our father drink wine, and we will lie with him, that we may preserve seed of our father.* [33] *And they made their father drink wine that night: and the firstborn went in, and lay with her father; and he perceived not when she lay down, nor when she arose,*
> (Genesis 19:30-33).

Is this not startling? Lot's daughters conspired to get their father drunk to be sexually intimate with him. Their reasoning was three-fold:

- There is not a man in the earth to come in unto us.
- Our father is old.
- To preserve seed of our father.

Wrong Motives

What caused the firstborn to say, ". . . there is not a man in the earth to come in unto us?" Recently, the three survivors of Sodom had traveled through the city of Zoar, where there were male residents. Clearly, Lot was not the only man alive.

Some other motive was at work. Had Lot's offer of his daughters to the men of Sodom awakened something perverse in the oldest daughter? Her reason for making this statement to her sister eludes rational thought.

If certain Jewish Rabbis are correct, Lot had moved to Sodom to participate in the perversion. Lot's oldest daughter conspired to take her father's misconduct to another level. And she intentionally used false information to convince her younger sister to join in the seduction of their father.

Lot had started a cycle of bad decisions. It often happens this way with a father's folly. Be careful of what you start.

When the girls plied him with drink, Lot became so intoxicated that he did not know when his oldest daughter came in or left. It is hard to imagine that come morning; Lot did not realize something sexual had happened. Should it not have raised Lot's suspicions?

On the next evening, Lot's daughters again kept his wine glass full. The outcome was the same.

> *And they made their father drink wine that night also: and the younger arose, and lay with him; and he perceived not when she lay down, nor when she arose.* (Genesis 19:35)

The Decision of the Second Night

Tolerate my thinking, please. What if Lot, after the first night, knew something sexual had transpired though he had been too drunk to know the specifics? Would Lot not have recalled being plied with wine? Conceivably!

The next day Lot's daughters whispered and giggled behind their hands. They had got away with it. So, the scheme was on again.

And on the second night, though perhaps suspicious about events of the previous night, Lot did nothing different. Again Lot's glass was never empty. The testimony of the second night: *Lot perceived not when his youngest daughter lay down nor when she arose.*

Was Lot foolish, naive, or a silent co-conspirator?

Lot's life was out of control. He had lost everything and was now repeatedly intoxicated. Lot's appetites often set aside his common sense.

No Escape from Reality

Intoxication seems to allow an escape from reality. Liquor, painkillers, heroin, cocaine, psychedelic drugs, sexual addiction, and ever-changing street-drug concoctions cause men to "lose their mind." Being "under the influence" causes life's difficulty to fade.

The problems may momentarily be forgotten, but they don't go away.

Lot's escape into memory-canceling intoxication only caused further difficulty. So it is for all escapism. Soon, the real world awaits.

Several things set the stage for Lot's daughters to behave as they did.

Casual Sex

Lot's daughters had lived in a city more liberal than our own culture. Sexual violence was routine.

The girls knew their father was casual about sexual matters. He had made them available to an angry mob. Lot not only devalued his daughters, but he also disrespected God's gift of sex.

With Lot as an example, it could be expected that his daughters would "act out." Lot's daughters lacked proper boundaries. They had no shame, even in committing incest with their father. Dad had treated sex as a casual thing, so they did the same.

Protect Your Family

We come back to the principle of providing your family a barrier against the degraded values of the world. How would protective barriers look?

1. Have frank discussions about sexual matters with your kids long before you think they need them. Plan for "the *ongoing* talk." If you don't educate your children, children on the playground, the school library, or the internet will.

2. Do not puritanical in addressing human sexuality. Sex is not evil. The misuse of physical intimacy is sin, but in marriage, the sexual relationship is a gift from God. Present sexuality to your children in a positive way.

3. Keep videos, books, and magazines that are sexually edgy out of your home. No wise man would invite his children to watch an X-rated video.

But don't overlook the attraction and misinformation that can come from the *Sports Illustrated* Swimsuit issue, *Argosy*, and thousands of books available at your library. If any media is rated "M" for mature, your children need YOU to protect their minds. Lot did not guard his daughters' minds.

4. Monitor what your child does online. Cell-phone carriers provide resources to control what your child can see and monitor what they have seen.

5. Open communication helps protect children. Tell your kids what sexual abuse is. Use words of medicine and science, rather than street language, but be sure they understand. Include in the discussion, "If anybody ever touches you in these ways or wants you to participate in anything that involves such, you are to tell me immediately. It does not matter who does it, whether it is Uncle Sammy or our neighbor, Bob. Nor should you believe what they say about you getting in trouble if you tell. You won't get in trouble, ever. And I will believe you."

Extremism

Lot was an extremist. He looked at well-watered plains and said, "It looks like the garden of God." But they didn't. The plains of the Jordan River look nothing like Eden.

Lot could have said, "I'll take the well-watered plains. That looks like an excellent place to raise livestock." But Lot had to make it seem like he was getting a super deal. Lot's talk was an exaggeration.

Parents are often extremists in how they deal with their children. This sort of extremism indicates immaturity and impatience. Extremists use common words:

- Always. You *always* give me the smallest piece of pie.
- Never. I *never* get to play outside.
- Every. *Every* car I buy is a piece of junk.

Lot's daughters were also extremists. The oldest of the two said, *"...there is not a man in all the earth to come unto us..."* (Genesis 19:31). It was an exaggeration.

The two girls were also impatient. Remember how Lot did not visit the well-watered plains to see them first-hand. His daughters acted similarly. They did not trek down to Zoar to see if eligible men were available.

No, like Lot, his daughters took quick action. They were immature and impatient. Don't give your children this as an example. There is a better way, cement this in your brain and let it guide your life:

> *For ye have need of patience, that, after ye have done the will of God, ye might receive the promise.* **(Hebrews 10:36)**

Think About It!

1. Lot's daughters conspired to involve their father in incestuous behavior. Think about Lot's earlier decisions that might have made these girls even think of such a thing. What should Lot have done differently?
2. We live in a time of great moral laxness. How do you plan to raise a "G" rated child in an "R" and "X" rated generation?
3. The sexual climate of our time does not differ much from Sodom. You are required to live surrounded by such. Lot chose his location. What can a father do to give his kids a chance of being saved?

Chapter 26
Decisions – as Sand Through an Hourglass

Some decisions are like a "Y" in the road. Will we go left or right; the direction we choose will set a course.

Other decisions are less sudden; they are like sand moving through an hourglass. The pull of gravity draws the sand, with the narrow neck limiting the pace of progress between the two glass globes. But with time, the sand inevitably moves downward.

Lot made some definitive decisions. But more significantly, with each choice, the gravitational pull toward Sodom's way of thinking and behaving was happening. Slowly but relentlessly, change came.

Patterns of Decline

Lot's pattern of decline may help to understand his behavior when faced with a threatening mob. If decades earlier, you had suggested to Lot, that he would offer his virgin daughters to the free use of rapists, Lot would have been furious with you. It might have come to blows.

Lot did not go from the company of Abram to making that sort of decision instantly. Lot was not an evil man; at least he did not begin that way. Peter even speaks of him as "righteous Lot."

Lot was, instead, a weak man. His fatal flaw, common in stubborn men, was an inability to recognize his vulnerability. Lot was a gullible man.

Lot would be the Dad who decided to move his family to a church that did not call for modesty and holiness. Ten years later, that father is shocked to see his daughters proudly posting pictures on social media of themselves wearing a tiny swimsuit while sipping a can of beer. Dear old "dumb," dad is angry and appalled. He later says to his daughter, "I can't believe you did that. You humiliated me. You were wearing fewer clothes than a street-walker." The sand has flowed through the hourglass!

Lot would be the man who practiced *Jesus Light*. He went to church once each month and had his wife bring their tithe. Then ten years later is scandalized that his child is attracted to Islam or Buddhism.

When subjects about the church or decent living come up in conversation, a man like Lot is surprised to hear his grown children say, "Dad, it's just religion. What does it matter?"

A Little Late

Such fathers are the guys who now want a pastor, a preacher - any preacher, to talk with his daughter about her lesbian lifestyle. Dad is desperate. But, through the years, he resisted every overture of the Spirit to draw him and his family toward godliness.

The book of Proverbs uses several antonyms for the word, *wise*. One such term is *simple*. A man is *wise* or *simple*, or some gradient of the two extremes. Lot was simple. In every decision, Lot was not wise. Not a single time! Never! From all we see, Lot did not have a wise bone in his body.

The Progression

Look at how a man became so unbalanced as to offer his daughters to angry rapists.

1. It began with a tentative commitment to faith and spiritual things.
2. Given the opportunity, he selfishly took advantage of others.
3. Without considering the negatives, he chose the well-watered plains of Jordan.
4. He "*tented*" toward Sodom.
5. He moved into Sodom.

6. Rescued from potential slavery, Lot returned to Sodom. Behavior that might once have scandalized Lot was now familiar.
7. As a resident of Sodom, he sought influence; he wanted to be a man sitting in the gate.
8. Lot offered his daughters to sexual predators to protect guests he scarcely knew.
9. Lot delayed his departure from Sodom.
10. Lot's wife made the one decision the Bible records. The result: she becomes a pillar of salt.
11. Lot argued for the preservation of Zoar. He did not want to travel too far.
12. Driven by fear, Lot left Zoar, taking his daughters further into the mountains where they took up residence in a cave.
13. Lot's daughters lived without boundaries because they had been taught no limits. They seduced their father.
14. Lot may have been oblivious the first night. On the second night, that seems doubtful.

Simple Lot conformed to the city around him. The Torah testifies that you cannot live near Sodom and remain unchanged. Lot let Sodom shape him, his wife, and children.

When The Sand Has Settled

Decades after leaving the company of Abram, Lot had no relationship with God. Lot also had no moral compass. The slow movement of sand was unavoidably complete. And, so it is for all who stay on such a path.

Think About It!

1. Remember an earlier decision that initially seemed simple; you made a choice, then matters seemed to take on a life of their own. Soon you were in a complicated situation. If you had an opportunity to make that decision again, what would you do differently?
2. Define the word: *wise*. There are many definitions. One "non-dictionary" definition of wisdom is: knowing what to do next! How does the word, *simple,* describe that which is the opposite of wisdom?
3. Do you know of someone for whom the sand flowed through the hourglass to the point that they no longer had any consideration of God in their life? Even in the worst of times? Can you recount the process whereby they came to such a state?

Chapter 27
The River of Lot's Decisions

When enough small choices flow together, they become a swift-moving river. Lot's bad decisions impacted history for centuries. As a result of seducing their father, Lot's daughters bore two sons, Moab and Benammi. Moab means "from the mother's father." Every person who met Moab would know him to be the result of incest.

Campfires before the Cave

In Lot's day, there was no written history. All history was orally passed from generation to generation. A story worth telling got retold often. And, Lot had stories to tell.

While Moab and Benammi grew up, the two boys learned of Lot's father and grandfather, of the majestic city of Ur, and the fantastic gardens in Egypt.

Lot's new young family was poor. But Lot's sons heard stories about his past wealth.

Though now in a cave, Lot's daughters told of the home they once had. During this same time, Abraham was increasingly wealthy, while Lot was poor. Poor kinfolk can speak ill of well-to-do family members.

How old were Moab and Benammi before they asked:

- Dad, what happened to all the sheep, goats, and cattle you once owned?
- Mom, why are we living in a cave? You told me about a beautiful home. Why aren't we living in it?
- Why isn't Momsie here? What happened to her?

And in time, the questions would have been answered.

They learned about their wealthy great uncle.

As children get older, they ferret out the family secrets. What did Lot tell his sons about Uncle Abram? When telling a story that involves ourselves, we protect our image. Lot blaming Abram for his situation is not logical, but blame needs no logic.

All Moab and Benammi heard were what their parents told them. It was one-sided. Wisdom dictates, even if it's your family member telling the story, never accept one person's account as "the story." It isn't! As an elder put it, "It's a mighty flat pancake that has just one side."

Likely, Lot did not speak highly of Abraham. Generations later, Lot's descendants showed a blatant hostility toward Israel. What Moab and Benammi heard from Lot, and their mothers became cornerstones in the oral history of the Moabites and Ammonites.

Over four-hundred years later, Lot's heirs seemed programmed to hate the descendants of Abraham. How could Lot not have hated his circumstances? Those unhappy with life tend to resent those who made better decisions, and Abraham had made the right decisions.

The root of bitterness can pass from generation to generation.

Think About It!

1. What family story did you know until you did some digging? Why did your family hide that story?
2. Were there any feuds in your neighborhood? One family hating another for generations? Did anyone ever tell you what started the feud?
3. What have you experienced that could be told in a way to cause your child to resent someone else? Why is it a bad idea to put such thoughts into your children?

Chapter 28
Moab – To Curse God's People

Moab's name forever marked them as people descended from incest. Would such an identity not have become a by-word? Can you envision the Moabites having a chip on their shoulder. The descendants of Lot certainly had enmity toward Israel.

When Israel traveled from Egypt to Canaan, Balak, the Moabite king, was frightened. Balaam, a "prophet," was hired to curse Israel. Balaam could not do it; every time he opened his mouth to speak a curse, a positive word came out (Numbers 22-24). By God's intervention, the Moabite intended evil became a blessing.

Moab's strategy changed. Advised by Balaam (Revelation 2:14), Lot's heirs tricked the Israelite men. The Moabite women lured them to "free and easy" sexual liaisons. Lot was willing to use his daughters to appease rapists. Centuries later, Moab's leaders used their women to seduce the Israelites.

After establishing an emotional connection, the Moabite women swayed the Israelite men to worship the false god Baal (Numbers 25:1-3). Baal well-matched Lot's descendants; extreme sexual excesses were part of Baal worship. It went beyond homosexuality and the sexual violence commonplace in Sodom and Gomorrah.

In dealing with Israel, what Lot's descendants could not curse, they seduced away from the Lord. The impact of Lot's bad decisions was now having implications on God's people.

Think About It!

1. Because of his name, imagine what conflicts the young man Moab might have experienced? How would a need to continually do battle have affected his descendants?
2. The Moabites never befriended Israel, though in the same neighborhood. Lot's decisions of long ago now troubled Israel. Do you know someone whose decisions produced a grudge

toward Jesus and His people? How is their animosity expressed?

Chapter 29
Deliverance from Moab

Any man who hopes to build his legacy on success or pleasure sows thorns in his family's future. Only by extreme personal intent does a family member escape the grasp of such a legacy. By God's grace and help, it can happen.

Your heritage may be one that is forgettable. Your father and those before him may have made decisions as Lot did. The impact of their focus on prosperity rather than faith has affected many. But, bad decisions need not be the legacy you leave behind. When you break free, the course of life for your descendants will change.

Ruth, who has a book in the Bible bearing her name, was a Moabitess. Ruth descended from Lot's oldest daughter and Lot. She came from the group who did everything they could to withstand Israel. Ruth is important.

- A book of the Bible carries her name. It is a fabulous story of redemption.
- Ruth was the great-grandmother of King David.
- Ruth, the Moabitess, is also in the genealogy recorded in Matthew 1.

Ruth descended from Lot, whose bad decisions are memorable, but she broke from her roots. Despite what had preceded her, Ruth made the right decisions.

How can a person break with their family's legacy of bad decisions, bitterness, failure, sin, and idolatry? Ruth managed to do it. You can do the same.

The Power of A Different Influence

Ruth came under the influence of a woman who knew about and talked oft the God of Israel. The woman was named Naomi. She was Ruth's mother-in-law and was originally from Bethlehem, a small village in Judah. Because of a famine, Naomi's family had migrated to Moab. Her son had married Ruth. Later Ruth's husband died, but Naomi still impacted Ruth's life.

Thankfully it was so. For Ruth to escape the legacy of Lot, she needed another influence. Naomi was the influence Ruth needed. Ruth *clave* to Naomi (Ruth 1:14).

Not only was Ruth's husband dead, but all Naomi's immediate family had died in Moab. Nothing remained to hold Naomi in this foreign land, so she decided to return to Bethlehem.

When Naomi returned to Israel, her future was uncertain. She has no money or kin on whom to depend. There was no assurance that things would go well.

Naomi did not leave Moab in the best state of mind; this showed when Naomi arrived in Bethlehem. Naomi asked the residents not to call her Naomi, which means *pleasant*. She told them instead to call her "Mara," a word that means *bitter*. While away from Bethlehem, Naomi had buried her husband and two sons.

Despite Naomi's grief and bitterness, her influence on Ruth became a change agent that would redirect Ruth's life.

Those wanting to escape a legacy from the past should find someone to be a godly influence. Do as Ruth. She *clave* to Naomi. Get as near a godly influencer as you can. Watch them, listen to them, and learn from them.

Commitment to the Journey

Notwithstanding Ruth knowing nobody in Bethlehem, Ruth said to Naomi, "*Where you go, I will go; and where you live, I will live,*" (Ruth 1:16). Nothing was certain – except uncertainty. But Ruth, Lot's descendant, who had lived in a culture still shaped by Lot's bad decisions, committed herself to the journey, wherever it led.

In Lot, such a commitment was absent. But by committing to the journey, whatever that entailed, Ruth changed her life. She also started another story entitled *The Legacy of Ruth*. *The Legacy of Ruth* has a much better outcome than *The Legacy of Lot*.

The difference, in part, is because of the decisions each person made. Lot was negligibly committed, while Ruth was totally committed.

A similar commitment to that of Ruth is required for any man to escape a legacy of bad decisions. Are you willing to follow the path of a disciple of Jesus Christ? There are no earthly guarantees of good health or wealth. However, it does provide the opportunity to be a positive impact and assurances for eternity.

Commitment to the Right People

Bethlehem was several days travel from Moab. Philosophically, culturally and religiously, the two places were several lightyears apart. In Moab, temple prostitution, sexual perversion, and violence were routine. Parents commonly sacrificed their firstborn children to idols. It had always been so with these descendants of Lot. What Lot, their grandfather many times removed, had decided for was no shock to Ruth's kin. It was the way of Lot.

For worship, the people of Bethlehem served one God. This God asked for no human sacrifices. Murder and sexual sin were against the law in Bethlehem. Instead of attempting to take advantage of others, the people of Bethlehem seized on opportunities to help the poor. The people of Bethlehem had a different set of values than those of Moab.

Change is accelerated when you spend time with the right people. Ruth told Naomi, *"Your people shall be my people"* (Ruth 1:16). Ruth relinquished her relationships in Moab.

Paul knew the impact of just spending time with the wrong people. He wrote, *"Do not be deceived: 'Evil company corrupts good habits,'"* (I Corinthians 15:33 NKJV). Ruth's old friends in Moab remained idol worshippers, surrounded by perversion and violence. Ruth wanted something different. If it were to be, she would need new friends.

Centuries earlier, Lot also decided. He chose Sodom – twice; Lot spent his time with vicious and perverse people. Lot led his family to the "wrong people." Ruth abandoned the legacy Lot's bad decisions had established.

A man wanting out of his version of *Moab* will prioritize time with other Christians, "Your people will be my people," is the declaration. It is vital for those who will leave a legacy of bitterness, resentment, and false gods.

Total Commitment to the Right God

Lot's descendants did not lack a god. Moab had "gods." Worship is always present. A god will be served. It may be idolizing dollars, sports, or power, but every man worships something. In Moab, Lot's descendants, worshipped Chemosh and Baal, among others. The adherents to these gods sacrificed infants and children.

Ruth made a decision. She said to Naomi, "Your God will be my God." Naomi had told of the promise to Abraham, the Exodus from Egypt, and of God's mercy to Israel.

Ruth did not bring trinkets honoring Chemosh or Baal with her. Her commitment to Naomi's God was absolute. "Your God will be my God," meant abandoning the liberty of polytheistic Moab. Ruth did not want to have the perversion and promiscuous freedoms of Baal in one hand and a relationship with Jehovah in the other.

Ruth committed to Naomi's God. He would be the one she loved with all her heart, soul, and might. Escaping the legacy of Lot is never casual.

Jesus Christ must be absolute in His Lordship. Nothing else will change the course of your life.

Think About It!

1. What do you suppose Naomi had said or done that caused Ruth to want her as a role model? Think about this from the perspective of influencing someone as Naomi had Ruth, what would you need to do?

2. Ruth had no assurance in Israel. Choices are made based on thinking something else is better. What did Ruth lose in departing Moab? What did she imagine herself gaining?
3. Ruth made three decisions, "Where you go, I'll go; your people will be my people, and your God will be my God." Why are these three things, such important decisions? In which of these do you find yourself repeatedly having to commit to doing the right thing?

Chapter 30
The Wins and Losses of a Man's Life

At season's end, each sports team has a won-loss record. It shows how well a team has done. A season's statistics show how each player has fared. Knowledgeable fans can know a player's effectiveness in seconds.

Statistics and the wins and losses evaluate an extended period. A player may have one exceptional game, but a terrible season. One game does not a season make. Short bursts of reliability do not overcome extended seasons of inconsistency.

Occasional moments do not evaluate a man's life. In music, some singers are called "one-hit wonders." They had one song on the charts and were never heard from again. Don't be a "one-hit wonder" for God, your family, your church, and the community.

In *The 7 Habits of Highly Effective People*, Steven Covey writes of the need to "Live with the End in Mind." Covey's readers do an exercise where they imagine their funeral. Several people speak at the funeral. Family members, co-workers, neighbors, and their pastor. Covey poses several thought-provoking questions:

- What do you want these people to say about you?
- Be honest, what would the speakers be able to say?
- What do you need to do for those who speak at your funeral to be able to say the things you want them to say?

Covey made his point. Being mindful of the end of your short season of life should help you make better decisions.

Look at Lot's Scorecard

- Lot followed Abram but continued only through coercion.
- Lot disrespected his neighbors and uncle.
- Lot moved his family to Sodom.

- His wife disobeyed the instruction of two angels and became a pillar of salt.
- His two older daughters and their husbands died in the fire and brimstone of God's judgment on Sodom and Gomorrah.
- Lot's two younger daughters got him drunk.
- In the drunken stupor, Lot's daughters seduced him.
- Lot's sons/grandsons were born to unmarried daughters.
- Lot's two sons, Moab and Ammon, were born of incest.
- Lot's last known address was a cave.
- At last sighting, Lot had no possessions beyond what three people could carry on their backs.
- Some of Israel's most consistent opposition came from the two nations Lot sired.

Because of Lot's bad decisions, did his descendants have a genetic predisposition to stand against the things of God? In what universe can Lot be considered a success?

Permissible Influences

Lot decided to have his family live in a setting rife with cruelty and perversion. Did "righteous Lot" think he could shield his family from Sodom's sway? A man who deliberately plunges his family into a culture of violent perversion is permitting the corrupting of his children.

Sexuality

Much of the world has validated "same-sex" marriage. The contrarian lifestyle has co-opted the word "gay." Christ, the Bible he was familiar with (Old Testament), and His Spirit-inspired apostles consistently condemn homosexuality.

But don't indict one sin as more damning than another. Sin is sin, and the Bible also condemns pre-marital sex, adultery, and living together outside marriage.

Our cups overflow with sexual language, media, and innuendo. Double-entendre is so common that it is now in Christian conversation.

Some "entertainment pulpits" use such words for shock-value. Such presenters imagine that their use of vulgarity and sexual entendre to present *easy-believism* makes them "cool, hip, modern, and in." They are wrong. Instead, it means they decided to join Lot in Sodom.

Violence

Brutality was also part of Sodom's identity. Lot's neighbors wanted to violate his guests. The outcome would be great physical harm.

Violence is "in." Within the past decade, a study of twenty-five years of movies discovered that 90% of those rated PG-13 or R had at least one lead character who was extremely violent. ("Violence in Movies Prevalent Whether its PG-13 or R." *CBSNEWS.Com*. December 9, 2013. Web. August 16, 2020)

Horror stories, action movies, and video games are full of gore. In video games, the blood spurts as pre-adolescents "shoot" other competitors. Is there any wonder that the murder rate has increased among men under 40? We have normalized violence. Brutality is an acceptable response, no matter how minor the stimulus.

Protecting Your Family

This book comes back to repeat some themes. It is for emphasis and by intent. You cannot build walls high enough to protect your family from violence and sexuality. But don't be like Lot and open your family to these influences. There are steps a wise man can take to safeguard his family.

1. Don't allow a book, magazine, television show, streaming video, or video game in your home if its content is inconsistent with the teaching of Christ. Watching a "flick" with your teen that includes an unmarried couple "almost" having sex gives your silent approval to your teen having heavy "make out" sessions

and more. Lot decided to move to Sodom. You are too smart to have ever done that. Now be wise – don't bring immoral visitors from Sodom to your home.

2. Violent video games put your kids at risk. Dartmouth research affirmed that such games make teens more aggressive. The study also found that teens who play risk-glorifying video games are more likely to later engage in high-risk behavior.

   This conduct included experimenting with alcohol, drugs, and risky sex. Violent video games also affect how teenagers see themselves. ("New Study: Video Games and Teen Behavior." *Dartmouth.edu*. Dartmouth. August 4, 2014. Web. August 16, 2016.)

   Don't turn your sons into wimps, but there is a difference between an eleven-year-old playing a deer-hunting game and a game where he is the villain against others in a portrayal of bloody gore.

   Be cautious about what you allow into your home. Do your best to know what is in your home.

3. Be willing to say, "No," repeatedly. Why stream a movie that portrays sexual coupling? Would you let people from the neighborhood enter your home, and act that way before your kids? Apply the same principle to what you rent or buy.

4. Consider putting a firewall on your internet service. It will restrict access to pornographic websites.

   Perhaps this is a struggle for you. How much do you want to get out of Sodom? Apps exist that give an instant report to an accountability partner if you try to go to a porn site.

A word in everyday use is "intentionality." Be intentional in thinking about long-term risks. Look beyond the foreground of a family night enjoying a funny movie, albeit a film that you've heard to be a bit risqué. Look into the distance, what impact will your decision to fellowship with the risque' have on your family. Don't follow Lot. Be a protector!

Think About It

1. What have you allowed in your home over the past six months that you would not have wanted to watch if Jesus were present beside you? Isn't His spirit within you? Did the Holy Ghost leave you while you watched that immortality?
2. Do you need to build a bonfire to destroy some music, videos, books, and magazines?
3. Are you paying attention to what your children are doing? Do you have access to their phones, tablets, and computers? You should. Even pre-adolescent children receive requests for nude pictures.
4. Don't assume your child is a paragon of virtue because they sing in the youth choir, are on the Bible Quiz team, or help with church hospitality. Be proactive! Assume the world, flesh, and Satan want to influence your child. In so thinking, you think correctly.

Chapter 31
The Decisions Never End

Lot decided to go with Abram. On another day, Abram had to insist Lot continue the journey. Lot initially decided for spirituality and faith, and then changed his mind.

Each day offers multiple opportunities to change your mind.

- A change in college degree programs is a decision.
- The decision is made to relocate.
- A different career is chosen.
- To attend church or go to the lake, for the third Sunday in succession – requires a decision.
- Financially supporting the church is a decision repeated with each pay period.

A man decides to follow Jesus, and his life is changed. His family is affected positively. Then the man decides to redirect his life. He backslides. The outcome is often tragic.

How might Lot's family history differ if he had maintained his commitment to Abram's faith and spirituality?

When the opportunity came, Lot separated from Abram. Fellowship ended. Lot would never again hear the story of Jehovah's call.

Lot had decided to go a different direction than Abram!

Positive Daily Decisions

Our daily decisions can be positive, neutral, or negative. It often takes years to prove the wisdom or folly of our choices. Time tests all decisions. Lot's selection of the well-watered plains seemed right. Perhaps it would have been, but those plains were the next step toward Sodom. Ensuing centuries proved Lot's folly.

Many decisions are beneficial. Improving your diet, starting a fitness program, increasing your knowledge, whether at college or through self-education, are all great decisions. We can quickly make such positive decisions, but they are enacted only by daily effort.

Bad decisions are also cumulative. Lot's small actions accumulated into ruin. *Tenting* toward Sodom, *disrespecting* his neighbors in daily business, and *selfishly* not considering Sodom's influence on his daughters determined who Lot was. Lot's greatest wrong was in the way he chose to live each day. His priorities were misplaced.

Men seek sudden success. We would like to imagine that by doing a grand or heroic thing, life's outcome would be settled. But that is not how life works. You must stay consistent in your <u>daily</u> commitment to Jesus Christ, your family, and your church.

The Normal Conflict

It seems likely that Lot wanted to have the best of both worlds. Desiring "more" in this way is not unusual. Long before Lot chose the well-watered plains, he was following a different course than Abram.

Lot's inner motivations, unveiled over time, were wealth, success, position, power, identity, and pleasure. Lot's fierce drive made him single-minded. The collateral damage to Lot's choices was of no concern to him.

Men who have pursued the spiritual, but later find themselves hotly chasing something else become blind to how they injure others. It is as though they wear blinders. Jesus said it:

No man can **serve two masters***: for either he will hate the one, and love the other; or else he will hold to the one, and despise the other. Ye cannot* **serve** *God and mammon,* (Matthew 6:24).

Lot's actions showed who he loved. Your decisions do the same. Since you can't serve two masters, make a firm commitment for Jesus; then support that commitment with your daily behavior.

Commitments a Man Should Make

1. Commit to a local church. Attend church, and if you must be absent, let your pastor know. If possible, watch or listen to any message you miss.
2. Commit to having moral integrity.
3. Put your wife and family on YOUR calendar. Schedule family outings, dates with your wife, father-daughter "dates" and father-son outings. Do not cancel these calendared events for "other things."
4. Practice having daily devotion. Find an approach to the "quiet times" with God that fits you.
5. Grow! Be a "lifelong learner." Apply this in your career, family responsibilities, and Christian living. Never stop learning about the things of God.
6. Give God a tithe (10%) of your increase. Add an offering to your tithe. Offering and tithe are not the same. They serve different purposes.
7. Commit to repeatedly making the right decisions. Each day is a new day. At each "Y" in the road, decide that you will be a good husband, father, grandfather, employee, boss, and Christian.

Think About It!

1. Lot pitched his tent toward Sodom. Thus began what may have been a slow movement toward Sodom. Have you seen a man start down a bad path and consistently stay on that course? Why do men continue doing something that seems to hold little promise?
2. A call to commitment is made. Which areas do you see as the biggest challenge for men overall? Is there an area that is the biggest challenge for you? Why?

Other Material by Carlton L. Coon Sr.

Carlton and Norma Coon co-pastor Calvary United Pentecostal Church in Springfield, Missouri. Audio of the preaching and teaching is available at SpringfieldCalvary.church.

Regular blog posts can be received by signing up at CarltonCoonsr.com

Ministry Monday is a short, relevant video provided each Monday on Facebook and as a YouTube channel. Ministry Monday is intended as a benefit to those involved in the "five-fold ministry." *Ministry Monday with Carlton Coon* is also available as a podcast on ITunes and other similar channels.

For Men – The God's Men Series

Distinctly Different

Distinctly Different – The Leader's Guide

Bad Decisions – The Legacy of Lot

Bad Decisions – The Leader's Guide

Good Decisions 31-Day Devotional

The Keep It Simple Saints (K.I.S.S.) Series

Personal Devotion

Broad Readership

Daily Things of Christian Living

If Everybody Here Were Just Like Me . . . (What kind of church would this church be?)

Healthy Church . . . Start Here!

Light in a Dark Place

Disciple-making and Church Growth

Disciple-makers Training Course – (Online)

Ten – The First Ten Days Of New Life

Take Root – Teacher and Student

Bear Fruit – Teacher and Student

Fitly Framed CD

You Wouldn't Want an Ostrich for Your Mama

How and Why of Hospitality -

How and Why of New Convert Care

How and Why of Follow-up

What the Bible Says (also available in **Spanish**, **French** and **Tagalog**.)

For Preachers

Until He Comes – Eight Lessons and Sermons on Communion

Masterful Preaching – Restoring the Place of Good News Preaching

Honey from a Strange Hive – Funeral Sermons

Questions Pentecostal Preachers Ask -

Beating the Marriage Busters – 7 lessons for Marrieds.

Biblical Parenting – 7 lessons on Parenting

Ephesians – To the Praise of His Glory (A series of ready-to-teach lessons)

The Details Matter: Principles and Practice of Church Administration

Order from:

    Carlton Coon Sr.

    4521 North Farm Road 165

    Springfield, MO 65803

Website: CarltonCoonSr.com

Made in the USA
Columbia, SC
08 July 2025